A MIGHTY RIVER

The Holy Spirit:

The Greatest Gift

Ever Given To The Church

by Michael Chorey

A MIGHTY RIVER

The Holy Spirit: The Greatest Gift
Ever Given To The Church

Editors: Kim Ashker, Julie Carey, Jane Carlsen,
Brian Rosman

Cover Design by Rick Mills

A publication of Joshua Revolution
256 Third Street, Suite 10
Niagara Falls, New York 14303
(716) 284-8173

www.joshuarevolution.org

A MIGHTY RIVER

The Holy Spirit: The Greatest Gift
Ever Given To The Church

Many Christians do not understand how the Holy Spirit works, what grieves, quenches, hinders, or moves the Spirit. "A Mighty River" will take you into the Scriptures to teach how the greatest gift the Lord has ever given His Church operates. When the believer understands the function, agency and operation of God the Holy Spirit, then this Mighty River will flow in his life.

"A Mighty River" is the sequel to the book CrossEyed, also written by Michael Chorey. It is recommended that you read both books, as the Cross and the Spirit work in unison. The two cannot be separated.

Table of Contents

Today, in the Church, we can observe two different extremes that have caused a lot of confusion and damage to the Body of Christ. On the one side, we have a conservative faction which has said that the gifts of the Holy Spirit have ceased, or are not for today. On the other side of the aisle we have what we will call the "charismatic faction" which has said that it believes in the gifts of the Spirit, but has gone into fanaticism with them. Both sides have grieved the Spirit of God and caused great damage to the work of God.

In this book, A Mighty River, we want to bring clarity to who the Holy Spirit is, and how He functions. We want to take a look at the early church and how it operated and moved in the Holy Spirit because we dare not limit, hinder or go beyond what the scriptures teach as to how the Holy Spirit works.

When I first got saved, I attended a church where, if someone raised his hand in service to praise the Lord, it would be considered a strange manifestation. It was very conservative in nature, and although the pastor – and most of the church – loved God, they were not expressive in the way they worshipped God. Why? Some would say that was just their style of worship. However, could there be a bigger reason, a more spiritual reason, as to why they were so reserved in their outward expression of worship for God?

As a new believer, I would visit churches that would be labeled Pentecostal or Charismatic and I would see a different expression in these churches. I would see outward emotion, be it dancing, shouting, raising of hands, etc. Was this just their personality, more bold and outward, or was this birthed by the Holy Spirit?

In my quest to learn about the moving and operation of the Holy Spirit, I began to study these two expressions. I would learn that the dividing line between these two forms of worshipping God was a matter of what each side believed about the Baptism with the Holy Spirit.

The conservative church believed that when you got saved, you got it all, but the Pentecostal church believed there was a subsequent encounter with the Holy Spirit after salvation that resulted in receiving the gift of tongues.

I found the biggest controversy in the church regarding these two sides was over the gift of speaking with other tongues. One side said it ceased at the dying of the first century apostles and the other side said that it was still for the believer today.

I do not believe this is some meaningless side issue that has no relevance to the believer today, but this important distinction means the difference of walking in the power of the Holy Spirit or grieving and quenching all that the Holy Spirit wants to do in, and through, the believer today.

As a college student in 1982, after I got saved I got hungry to learn more about the Holy Spirit. I wanted to know what the Bible taught regarding the third person of the Trinity. I didn't want to go with a denominational tradition or teaching, whether it be conservative or charismatic, but I wanted to know and live by what the Word of God taught. I thought to myself, I can't be wrong on this, I have to know the truth as Jesus said, "*You shall know the truth and the truth shall make you free*" (John 8:32).

What is the truth of the Holy Spirit? Are His Gifts still in operation today? Is He still working through believers to heal the sick? Is He still baptizing believers with His Holy Spirit with the evidence of speaking with other tongues? Is He still using believers to cast out devils?

This is not about having experiences that are extra-biblical, but it's about Bible-based, Cross-centered truths that cannot be ignored any longer. The Book of Acts is one of the 66 books of the Bible, and it teaches us how the Holy Spirit worked in the early church and how He still works today.

In this book, we will look at what the Bible says, and I will share with you the incredible ways God has shown me His power for nearly 30 years of walking with Him and being in ministry. What I have learned is His power is real, and He is still baptizing believers with the Holy Spirit today. If you have been told otherwise, then you have been lied to, and your spiritual potential has been limited. However, if you have been led into the gifts of the Spirit without the foundation of the cross, then you have been led into error, and probably into emotionalism and extremism as well.

We are living in a time where the return of Christ is very soon and we must return to biblical Christianity. We must not water down, take away from, or add to the Word of God.

The church that is eagerly awaiting her Bridegroom to come can no longer ignore the mighty attributes of the Holy Spirit. We have been deceived by the devil long enough. The devil knows that if we ever believe in what the Bible says about the Mighty River of the Holy Spirit, then we will begin to see a demonstration of the Spirit just like they saw in the early Church. In fact, that demonstration is already happening – but sadly, in too few places.

I hope you are hungry for more of God, because you can never exhaust His attributes. I hope you are ready to experience the Mighty River of God. He only works through faith in what Jesus did, and this book is a Cross-centered, Cross-eyed approach to learning about the Holy Spirit. I pray that what you are about to read will either bring you back to where you once were, confirm where you are or bring you into a whole new place in your relationship with God. Get ready to learn about and experience the Mighty River of God!

Chapter 1

My Initial Experience With The Holy Spirit

C&E Christians

It was Christmas Eve 1978, and my family was getting ready for our traditional Christmas Eve family celebration. My mom was busy cooking the meal, my sisters were wrapping gifts, and my dad was out buying his last minute Christmas presents for the family. He always waited until Christmas Eve to do his shopping. Dad said it made Christmas more exciting.

We were not a very religious family. We simply lived our lives with a mentality of believing in God, but thought that we could live however we thought was best. We had little knowledge of what the Bible said in terms of having a personal relationship with God.

So my family (although we believed in God) was lost, and if we had died at that time, I believe we would have spent eternity in hell. But even though we were lost and without Jesus, we held to tradition and attended church on Christmas Eve and Easter (Resurrection Sunday). You could say we were C & E Christians. We were not born again, but we acknowledged the two most important seasons of Christianity.

Due to busyness that particular Christmas Eve, none of my family decided to attend the Christmas Eve service. The old saying is true: "If the devil can't make you bad, he will make you busy." We were so busy celebrating the holiday that we forgot who the holiday was all about. We didn't understand that Jesus is the reason for the season.

Christmas is all about when Christ was born to save a sinner such as me. The angels proclaimed on that first Christmas Night, *"Fear not: for, behold, I bring you good tidings of great joy, which shall be to all the people. For unto you is born this day in the city of David a Savior which is Christ the Lord"* (Luke 2:10-11). Even from the first moment Jesus came into this world His purpose was determined: to be "a Savior." Jesus was born to die that we might live.

Jesus was born in a small town called Bethlehem. The name Bethlehem means "house of bread." Jesus referred to Himself as the "Bread of Life" (John 6:48). He is the Bread that feeds a hungry soul. The Bible tells us that when Jesus was born, He was born in a stable because there was no room for Him in the inn (Luke 2:7). That was where my family was in 1978 - we were too busy on Christmas to make room for Jesus. Our family was celebrating a holiday which we really did not understand the true meaning of. But for some reason that Christmas Eve I just knew I had to go to church. I guess I didn't want to break tradition, or maybe I thought it would be bad luck. Whatever my reason was, in my heart it wasn't right for me to skip Christmas Eve service.

There was a little church around the corner from our house called Grace Parkridge Church, and it was the place my family would go whenever we attended church. Even though I only went a couple times a year, I remember I loved to go on Christmas Eve. There was always a huge tree at the altar decorated with beautiful Christmas lights. They would pass out candles to each person, and we would all sing "Silent Night" at the conclusion of the Christmas Eve service.

As I prepared to go, I remember Mom apologizing and saying she was disappointed that I had to go alone. I assured her that it was fine and that I knew she had a lot to prepare for the Christmas Eve party later that night, which was a custom at our house every year. My mom is a terrific cook and a great hostess, and everything had to be just right for our guests.

Silent Night, Holy Night

When I arrived at the church, I must admit, it felt strange to sit alone when everyone else seemed to be with their families. I had an image in my neighborhood of being tough, so I felt a little self-conscious sitting there all alone. Nonetheless, something just felt very right about me being there. The usher welcomed me as he handed me a church bulletin and gave me a candle. I was so glad that they were holding to the tradition of lighting the candles and singing Silent Night. I seemed to wait the whole service in anticipation of that moment.

As the preacher gave his Christmas message, I observed all the children with their parents and thought, "I wish my family was here with me." I had a sense in my heart that I was in the right place, and that God was pleased by my decision to come to church on Christmas Eve.

Then came the anticipated moment when they lit the candles and began to sing. As I sat there and listened to the sound of many voices singing Silent Night, Holy Night, I felt a deep love come over me. I began to get choked up and I couldn't hold back my tears. I grew up in an inner-city neighborhood where it wasn't cool to show your emotions publicly - especially about God - so I was a little self-conscious at that moment, to say the least.

When the song finished, the people extinguished the candles and the church lights came back on. I quickly wiped the tears from my eyes, as I didn't want anyone to know that I was crying. The preacher said his closing words and dismissed the congregation. I was anxious to exit the church because I didn't want anyone to see me, as I felt a little guilty for hardly ever attending church. The fact that I was by myself made me feel even more vulnerable.

However, people were standing in line to leave, creating a bottleneck, at the door. I wondered why the line was moving so slowly, but as I moved closer to the door I saw the reason. It was the Pastor, Rev. McCready, who was shaking hands with each person. I really started getting nervous then, thinking he hasn't seen me in church in a long time (probably since Easter), and what would he say when he saw me? I had made my communion when I was 13, but never followed through with my commitment. I wondered if he would chastise me for not coming to church.

When I finally got to the door, there he stood, towering over me. He was a tall man, at least 6'4". He reached out his very large hand to shake mine and when I put my hand into his, it seemed as though it got lost. I looked up at him for a brief moment, not knowing what he was going to say to me. To my surprise, he had a loving smile on his face and said something to me that really shocked me. He said: "Merry Christmas, Michael." I couldn't believe he remembered my name. I quickly responded "Merry Christmas, Reverend." Even though I was almost never in church, he treated me that night as if I was a regular attendee. He moved my heart with his greeting as I quickly slipped out the door into the cold winter's night. I felt a sense of freedom once I was outside, thinking the conviction that I felt inside the church would now leave me.

The Spirit of Christmas

As I began my short walk home, I noticed how amazing the Christmas night was. The gently falling snow had beautiful sparkling crystals and the houses were lit with glittering lights. As I came around the corner from Parkridge onto Dunlop Avenue (the street I lived on), I observed the beauty of Christmas Eve with an unusual sense of peace. Then, all of sudden, something happened that I would remember for the rest of my life.

A tremendous wave of love came crashing over me and instantly tears began to roll down my cheeks. I had goose bumps all over my body, but and it wasn't from the cold night. There was a warm presence that met me on that Christmas Eve that was undeniable. I didn't know how to explain it to my family, so I never told them. In my mind, I described it as the Spirit of Christmas, but I would learn later that it was my first encounter with the Holy Spirit.

In the Bible, a man named Saul (who opposed Christians) was journeying to Damascus, and suddenly a light from heaven flashed around him and he fell to the ground and heard a voice speak to him and say, *"Saul, Saul, why are you persecuting Me?"* This is recorded in Acts 9:1-12 (NAS) and it is the famous conversion of the Apostle Paul, the man God would use to write nearly one-third of the New Testament. Paul, not realizing who had spoken, said, *"Who art Thou, Lord?"* And the voice said to him, *"I am Jesus whom you are persecuting."*

Even though I didn't hear God's voice, like Saul, I was having my first God-encounter. Even though I wasn't persecuting Christians as Saul was, I still was a foul-mouthed sinner who didn't pay much attention to God. But that night God invaded my life by His Spirit, and He reached out His hand from heaven to me. The Bible says, *"Behold, the Lord's hand is not shortened, that it cannot save"* (Isaiah 59:1).

This encounter with God, which at the time I wouldn't have even described as such, was God's initial approach toward me finding Jesus as my personal Lord and Savior. It would take four more years before I would accept the Gospel message, but I know now that on Christmas Eve in 1978, God met me on that road and He reached out His hand and touched me in a real way. The presence of His Holy Spirit was real and this first encounter was one that I would never forget.

A few years later, my sister Karen would receive the Lord, and she would be the first person in my family to become "born again."

What does it mean to be "born-again"? It is a phrase first uttered by Jesus, recorded in the Gospel of John, Chapter 3. Nicodemus, a Pharisee went to see Jesus. Jesus told Nicodemus *"Except a man be born again, he cannot see the kingdom of God"* (John 3:3) The priest thought Jesus was referring to a physical second birth. Jesus explained to him, saying *"Except a man be born of water and of the Spirit, he cannot enter into the kingdom of God"* (John 3:5). The reality of sin hits the lost soul as he is convicted and brought to faith in Jesus Christ and what He did for him on the Cross. He invites Jesus to come into his heart; and it is the Holy Spirit, according to faith and repentance (Mark 1:15), who enters the sinner's heart. At that moment the person is considered "born again" or "born of the Spirit." A new life then begins, one that is in relationship with Jesus Christ through the power of the Holy Spirit, who is now living in the believer's heart.

Jesus gave even more explanation of what it means to be born again when He said to Nicodemus, *"the wind blows where it wishes and you hear the sound of it, but do not know where it comes from, and where it is going; so is everyone who is born of the Spirit"* (John 3:8).

You can't see the Spirit entering because He is invisible. However, you will see the effects of the Spirit coming in as you begin to exhibit a lifestyle of love for God, a love for the things of God, and a desire to live in right-standing with Him. You will be in submission to the holiness of God, whereas before you may not have cared or just gave very little thought about it.

So, there are two births that can take place. First, the birth of the flesh as one comes into this world, and then, the birth of the Spirit (John 3:6) which allows the person to enter into the next life - life eternal with God in Heaven. Any person who is not born of the Spirit will go to an eternal hell, spending forever where there is weeping and gnashing of teeth (Matthew 8:12). The born again experience is available to all, for God so loves the world (John 3:16) and He is not willing that any should perish (II Peter 3:9).

After my sister was saved, she instantly began to share Christ with our family. The supernatural working of the Holy Spirit brought my family to the Lord. Just as I experienced on that Christmas Eve, the God of the universe is a personal God and He can bring His presence upon us at anytime. It would take much work and patience from my sister and my family, but I would come to the same conclusion that they had come to: Jesus is real and I needed Him.

God is a Personal God

As my sister Karen would spend many hours with me listening and witnessing to me about God's love, I was intrigued by this "born again" stuff. However, there were times when I thought my family members had all lost their minds, especially my mom. When Mom came to Jesus, she instantly became a fanatic. I mean, she would be in her Bible sometimes until four o'clock in the morning. She would say to me she couldn't sleep, that she had to keep reading the Bible. All she talked about was Jesus. Karen seemed to be a little more in control, but she was loving what God was doing in my mom's life, not to mention my dad and my sister Linda, who had also come to the Lord and were all going to church every Sunday.

When my mom started praying for me to give my life to Jesus, I didn't know it then, but I didn't have a chance: it would only be a matter of time. I can remember that for a six-month period before receiving Christ, everything I did failed. I couldn't even win a card game. My whole life felt like one big failure. I remember thinking, "I am the biggest loser and

I can't do anything right." Now I know that the devil wanted to destroy my life, but God was answering Mom's prayers. She was praying "God, whatever it takes, bring my son to You."

I used to think that only weak and defeated people became Christians, and if I gave my life to the Lord, that would be a sure sign of weakness. My pride had taught me to be a self-made man, independent and able to fix my own problems. This same mentality has sent countless millions of people to an eternal hell.

I believe most people who come to Christ must come to the end of themselves and realize they are moral failures, meaning they have failed God and failed to obey all of His commandments. The realization that every person must come to is:*"all have sinned, and come short of the glory of God"* (Romans 3:23). My sister Karen, in a loving way, was pointing this out to me, but I was rebellious and had to learn the hard way.

I can remember at times I couldn't take all the Christian music in the house always blaring, so I would go into my room and turn on my Rick James album, "Super Freak." I would go with my friends to the bars, but I always had this sense in my heart that Mom was praying for me and it wouldn't be long before I became like them. So I rebelled all the more. Thank God for His mercy, that He protected my life in my time of rebellion.

The Power of a Mom's Prayer

My life got really bad while I was in college. I didn't like my major, my athletic career was in shambles, I was drinking heavily, I was depressed over broken dreams and felt a giant hole in my heart that I couldn't fill, all the while living in a home with a bunch of Jesus freaks. I was surrounded. I didn't have a chance to escape my mom's prayers! Praise God!

I finally gave into my family's wishes and decided to go to church with them. I didn't go every Sunday, but just when my hangover from the night before wasn't too bad.

My family now attended a fairly big church. I really enjoyed the preacher, as his messages spoke to my heart and I knew God was speaking to me. But there was something the preacher would do at the end of every message that I really disliked. He would call people to come forward and give their lives to Jesus. He asked them to pray what he called the "sinner's prayer," inviting Jesus to come into their lives and become their personal Savior. This really bothered me because I thought, "I don't have to go forward in front of all these people. I can pray right in the quietness of my own heart. I mean, this is a personal decision between me and God." So, each week (or whenever I infrequently went to this church), I would say the "sinner's prayer" in my heart sitting in the pew, but I would not go forward.

Each time, however, I would walk out of the church and nothing would change. I would continue with my sinful lifestyle. But Mom kept praying and my sister kept witnessing. It got to a point that my own personal life got so bad that I was convinced there was a curse on my life. I felt like I couldn't shake it.

I finally decided that I had to give my life to Jesus: it was the only answer. I remember looking at the calendar and seeing that my 20th birthday landed on a Sunday and was only a few weeks away, so I decided that I would give my life to Jesus on my birthday.

I remembered thinking, "I only have a few weeks left, I need to party hard because it is shortly coming to an end." I knew, based on what my sister had told me and what I had viewed in my family, that coming to Jesus wasn't just a prayer but it was a dedication of your whole life. Becoming a Christian meant repenting of your sins (Acts 2:38).

People who say they believe in Jesus, but have not given their whole lives to serving Him, must realize they have just an intellectual belief. Mere intellect will not save you. The Bible says, *"Even so faith, if it hath not works, is dead, being alone"* (James 2:17). True faith always requires action. To become "born again," the Holy Spirit (God's Spirit) must come into your heart; and the only cry that the Holy Spirit will respond to is a cry from the heart that says "Jesus, I want to give my life to you."

Reggie Dabbs, a very popular youth evangelist, says it this way, "Jesus died for you, and He wants to now live in you." I knew by looking at my family that being a Christian was more than mental belief, or simply saying the "sinner's prayer." Becoming a Christian meant living an entirely different way.

Finally Sunday, March 28, 1982 came, and throughout the whole service I was waiting for the time when the preacher would call people forward to commit their lives to Christ. I had made up my mind that I was going to do it, although the whole time it seemed as though the devil was trying to keep me from going forward. The preacher got to that moment, and he said these words that I will never forget. He said, "Jesus went all the way to the Cross for you; you can certainly come this short distance for Him." However, it wasn't the distance that was intimidating me, but it was going in front of everyone.

In my mind, I always thought that people who gave their lives to Jesus needed a crutch. But now after several months, even years of failure and emptiness, I knew my life was broken, that I needed a crutch to lean on, and I knew in my heart that Jesus was that crutch.

The moment had arrived, and it seemed like all of hell was screaming "don't do it." With all the courage I could muster, I arose from my pew; it was just like the preacher said - the first step was so hard, but the rest were so easy, because with the first step I was making my commitment.

I truly believe Jesus Christ came into my heart the moment I stood to my feet. When I reached the aisle, I felt like running to the altar. I didn't know what Mom and Dad were experiencing back in the pew, but I am sure there were tears in their eyes as their prayers were answered; their son was repenting of his sins and was dedicating his life to Jesus.

When I reached the altar, I looked up and the preacher asked me, "Why have you come forward?" I thought if I answered this wrong, I might be damned to hell forever. I felt the presence of the Holy Spirit as I stood there with tears in my eyes, and I said the first thing that came to my mind, "Because I love Jesus." The preacher smiled and said, "That's the right answer."

It had been over four years since my first encounter with the Holy Spirit on that snowy Christmas Eve. But the big difference was: the Holy Spirit came upon me in 1978, but now He was coming to live inside of me.

Jesus said:

"And I will pray the Father, and He shall give you another Comforter, that he may abide with you for ever. Even the Spirit of truth; whom the world cannot receive, because it seeth Him not, neither knoweth Him: but ye know Him; for He dwelleth with you, and He shall be in you." (John 14:16- 17)

At the moment that I went forward to give my life to Jesus, something so miraculous, so extraordinary, happened that my human vocabulary fails to express the change that I encountered in the days that followed.

Born Again

After going forward in that Sunday morning service, the preacher directed me to a room where an altar worker prayed with me and handed me some materials that he said would help me in my new relationship with Jesus Christ. He took some information from me, and when he asked me what my date of birth was, I told him and he wrote it down and then he looked at me and said, "Wait a minute, today is your birthday!"

For 20 years of my life I lived for myself, and now it was time to begin a new life - a life that would be dedicated to living for Jesus. Although the "born again" experience will change a person's life forever, it doesn't mean that you will not sin again or you will not encounter any more problems. The truth is, the Christian experiences difficulties, sometimes even more so than the non-Christian, due to the fact that the world doesn't take kindly to someone who is deeply in love with Jesus and is not afraid to share it.

The new birth is a supernatural experience whereby the Holy Spirit, the Mighty River, comes into the heart of the believing sinner. The Bible tells us, regarding this experience, that *"he is a new creature: old things are passed away; behold, all things are become new"* (II Corinthians 5:17).

When I went to the back of the church after the service, my mom and dad were waiting for me, and I felt like a brand new person. My sins were gone, and the heaviness of living in guilt and rebellion was gone, too. My mom and dad looked at me with such joy as my mom handed me a gift. I didn't know what it was, but I quickly opened it up. It was my first Bible and my name was embossed on the front cover.

There was also a round magnet that Mom had glued onto the cover that said, "God will answer prayer." That day He certainly did for my mother, as she told me she had bought that Bible some time ago. Every week whenever I would decide to go to church with them, she would sneak that Bible into the car and put it under the front seat, praying and hoping that would be the week that I would give my life to Jesus. Well, her prayers were answered!

I instantly began to read that Bible and, to my surprise, I could understand it. I couldn't believe how much I loved reading the Bible. One of the most miraculous things that happened to me when I got saved was that I instantly fell in love with the Word of God and I could actually understand it when, just a day before giving my life to Christ, the Bible made no sense to me.

What most people don't understand is that the Bible is a spiritual book. It was not written with human intellect, and human intellect cannot comprehend it. Only the Spirit of Truth, the Holy Spirit, can bring revelation to the reader.

When the Holy Spirit comes in and gives the believing sinner the ability to understand the Bible, it is proof positive to the person that he has experienced the "new birth." I knew that something had drastically changed in my life, and it was that the Holy Spirit had come rushing in! God is real, and His Spirit is a mighty, life-giving River that was undeniable to me!

If you have never experienced the new birth in your life, I want you to know it can happen to you right now. All you need to do is surrender to Jesus Christ and believe that when He died on the Cross, He was doing it to pay the penalty for your sins. If you will repent (a change of mind) of your sins and turn your life over to Jesus, then He will come in and change you forever. I want to encourage you to say a simple prayer, but mean it with all your heart. Are you ready to experience the life-changing power of Jesus Christ? Then let's pray.

Heavenly Father, I come to you in Jesus' Name. I agree with Your Word that I am a sinner and I cannot save myself. Please forgive me for all of my sins. I want to turn from sin and live a life that is pleasing to You. I believe that Your Son, Jesus Christ, died on the Cross to pay the penalty for my sins. I believe He was buried and rose again so that I

could be saved from hell, have victory over sin and experience new life. So right now, by faith, I invite You, Jesus, to come into my life and be my personal Savior. According to Your Word (Romans 10:9), I confess with my mouth that You are the Lord of my life and I believe that you were raised from the dead so You could be alive in me. Jesus, please come into my heart right now by the power of Your Holy Spirit. I love You and I dedicate my life to living for You.

In Jesus' Name, I pray.

If you have just prayed this prayer and meant it with all your heart, you have the assurance of Romans 10:13 which says, *"Whosoever shall call upon the Name of the Lord shall be saved."* Your name has been written in the Lamb's Book of Life (Revelation 20:15). The Holy Spirit has come into your heart and will begin to work in your life as you continue to put your trust and faith in the finished work of Jesus Christ. The Mighty River can now begin to flow in your life!

Chapter 2

THE HOLY SPIRIT: THE GREATEST GIFT EVER GIVEN TO THE CHURCH

For over 4,000 years of human history, God dealt with man from the outside in. In the Old Testament, God, by His Spirit, would come upon man and give Him strength, guidance, miraculous power, wisdom, etc. Today, as believers, we are able to have a relationship with God that operates from the inside out through the gift of His Holy Spirit coming to dwell within us. Before we take a closer look at the work of the Holy Spirit in the believer's life and the Church as a whole, we need to have an understanding of how the Holy Spirit comes into and operates in the believer's life.

On Mt. Sinai, God spoke to Moses and gave Him the Law (the 10 Commandments) and then He gave Moses the exact details on how to build a Tabernacle where God's Glory would dwell. He told Moses that He would commune (which means to speak) with him from above the Mercy Seat and between the Cherubim (Exodus 25:22).

The Mercy Seat was in the Holy of Holies beyond the veil which separated the people from the presence of God. Only the High Priest, once a year on the Day of Atonement, could go beyond the veil and approach the Mercy Seat, and even then there were specific instructions to follow or else he could die. One must realize that God is a Holy God. Sinful man must approach God only as God directs and allows.

When one takes a closer look at the specifications that God gave Moses in building the Tabernacle, one will discover the important revelation of just how man can enter into a relationship with a thrice-holy God.

First, notice the location from which God said He would commune with Moses. He said, *"I will meet with thee, and I will commune with thee from above the mercy seat"* (Exodus 25:22). Why was this place, "above the Mercy Seat," so sacred to God?

The Greek word (which is the language the New Testament was originally written in) for "Mercy Seat" is "hilasterion" and it means "the place of sacrifice," where the blood was sprinkled in the presence God. The word for Mercy Seat has the same root as the word atonement. It means to cover, cancel, appease or cleanse.

The revelation of the Mercy Seat provides us with a picture of the only way God will commune with sinful man. Let's back up for a moment in this Tabernacle designed by God, and built by Moses accordingly.

The Tabernacle, which means "dwelling place," was like a church on wheels. What I mean by that is, it was built to move as the children of Israel moved across the desert. The presence of God was to dwell with them as they wandered in the wilderness for 40 years, en route to the Promised Land.

Upon entering the Tabernacle, the first thing you encountered was the "Brazen Altar." It was the place where the animals were offered up - slain (killed) for the sins of the people. The Brazen Altar is a type of the Cross of Calvary where Jesus died for all men for all time.

John the Baptist, the forerunner who prepared the way for the Messiah to come, said these words when he saw Jesus coming toward him at the Jordan River, *"Behold the Lamb of God, which taketh away the sin of the world"* (John 1:29).

Jesus Christ, on the Cross, was God's perfect Lamb who was offered once and for all for the sins of the world. Because of His shed blood, the Brazen Altar was put out of business. Praise God! No more innocent lambs had to be sacrificed for the sins of the people.

The Bible tells us that the High Priest in the Old Testament entered the Holy of Holies once a year, with blood from the Brazen Altar to sprinkle on the Mercy Seat. This, done on the Day of Atonement, was a type, or foreshadow, of what Jesus Christ would do on the Cross.

"Nor yet that he should offer himself often, as the high priest entereth into the holy place every year with blood of others; For then must he often have suffered since the foundation of the world: but now once in the end of the world hath he appeared to put away sin by the sacrifice of himself." (Hebrews 9:25, 26)

It is the blood of Christ that allows us to approach God and to have a relationship with Him. Without the blood of Christ, there is no forgiveness and there is no way man can experience the new birth. So, every man must go to the Brazen Altar, which is now the Cross of Christ, in order to commune with God and to be in a personal relationship with Him. There is simply no other way!

The Bible is clear, as it tells us over and over again that man can only approach God through the blood of Christ. Romans 3:25 says, *"Whom* (speaking of Christ*) God hath set forth to be a propitiation through faith in his blood."*

The word "propitiation" in the Greek means "lid or mercy seat." So, in other words, Christ and Him crucified is the Mercy Seat. This is one of the greatest revelations the child of God can ever learn. It tells us this is the place where God will enter into relationship with man. It is at the Mercy Seat, or in other words, at the Cross of Christ, that God meets with the sinner.

The devil will do everything in his power to keep the sinner from understanding this great truth and turning to the Cross. But, he also will work just as vehemently to keep the believer from staying at the Cross.

There are many believers in Christ today who love God, but are struggling to live for Him. In reality, they are failing God constantly and living a defeated Christian life, even though Jesus promised an abundant life. So, one must ask the question, "Why am I not experiencing victory? Why is sin controlling me?"

The answer to that question can be given in one simple way: the believer, whoever he may be, is living a defeated life because he has left the Cross. As a result, the Holy Spirit is not in control. He may admit that it is only the Cross of Christ that can save and provide eternal life. He may know he cannot earn his way to heaven. (These are basic Christian truths.) However, when it comes to living for Christ, his attempts fall short.

When the believer leaves the Cross, the devil has him. The Bible gives an incredible key to living the abundant Christian life, and it is found in Colossians 2:6, *"As ye have therefore received Christ Jesus the Lord, so walk ye in him."*

Did you get it? Did you see the truth here? How did you receive the Lord Jesus in the first place? By grace, through faith in what He did on the Cross to save you (Ephesians 2:8-9). Paul, writing under the inspiration of the Holy Spirit, is saying your walk with God, which means your everyday relationship with Him, is carried out in the same way that you first received Jesus Christ. You went to the Cross and believed what He did there for you and that, alone, set you free.

That is why Jesus said, *"If any man will come after me, let him deny himself, and take up his cross daily, and follow me"* (Luke 9:23). So, in essence, **don't leave the Cross, but carry it with you everywhere you go!**

What does it mean to "take up his cross daily?" The Cross has to be personal. It must be your Cross. This is speaking of what Jesus did there. The work of the Cross has to do with you dying to self and believing that He broke the power of sin's grip for you on the Cross.

God has forgiven us and cleansed us; He has paid our sin debt. We don't have to suffer the consequence of sin, which is spending eternity in hell. It also means that the power of sin over our life has been broken, so we don't have to live in bondage to sinful habits any longer. Where then is the boasting? There is none, only will I boast in the Cross (Gal. 6:14). Jesus did it all, and all I have to do is keep my faith in what He did and I will have the victory over the worldly lusts of my flesh (I John 5:4).

The Greatest Blessing of the Cross

As a result of what Jesus did on the Cross, the believing sinner can enter into a relationship with a Holy God. Now watch this – this is an "Ah Ha" moment! When Jesus Christ died on Calvary, something amazing happened in the Temple at Jerusalem.

The veil, which separated the people from the Holy of Holies, where God's presence dwelt and only the high priest could enter once a year, was ripped in two. This signified that there was no longer a separation – no barrier – for the child of God to enter into a personal relationship with Him. For the Bible says that when Jesus yielded up the ghost, which means He died by His own admission as no one took His life but He laid it down freely, at that moment the Word of God says, *"And, behold, the veil of the temple was rent (ripped) in twain from the top to the bottom"* (Matt. 27:51).

This ripping of the veil signifies that now the child of God can go boldly into the presence of God (Hebrews 4:16). There is only one condition and that is you have to first go through the Brazen Altar, which today is the Cross of Christ. After you have gone to the Cross and put your faith in Christ and what He did to cleanse you from your sin, now you are ready to be the recipient of the greatest gift ever given to mankind and that gift is the Holy Spirit.

The Cross paves the way for the Holy Spirit to be planted into your heart. In fact, the Cross, and faith in what Jesus did there for you, not only paves the way for the Holy Spirit to come into your heart and for you to have a relationship with God, but it is also what will keep the Holy Spirit moving in your heart and life.

In Galatians 4:6, the Bible says, *"And because ye are sons, God hath sent forth the Spirit of his Son into your hearts, crying Abba, Father."* The moment you invite Jesus Christ into your life through faith, the Spirit, speaking of the Holy Spirit or Spirit of Christ, will come into your heart and dwell there.

The word "heart" in the Greek is "kardia" and it means the deepest part of man, "the spiritual core." What an amazing miracle the new birth is. There is nothing like it in all of the world. The Holy Spirit, the Spirit of God, comes to live within the heart of man. Wow!

The Bible declares that when the believing sinner invites Christ to come into his heart, his body becomes the Temple of God, as soon as His Holy Spirit enters in. I Corinthians 3:16 declares, *"Know ye not that ye are the temple of God, and that the Spirit of God dwelleth in you?"*

In the Old Testament, God dwelt in the Tabernacle of Moses in the Holy of Holies, but today His Spirit lives in the heart of the man or woman, boy or girl, who puts his or her faith in what Jesus Christ did at Calvary and has invited Jesus to come into his or her heart.

The "new birth," which is experienced when the Holy Spirit comes in, is the greatest miracle and the greatest moment in a person's life. This experience is referred to in the Bible as "an operation." It actually is a spiritual operation when God the Father and His Son Jesus Christ, "the Great Physician," perform spiritual surgery on the heart of sinful man.

The Bible says we are, *"Buried with him* (speaking of Christ*) in baptism, wherein also ye are risen with him through faith of the **operation of God**, who hath raised him from the dead"* (Col. 2:12).

In the above verse, the apostle Paul (who wrote the Book of Colossians, inspired by the Holy Spirit) stated that the work of the new birth, our salvation experience, is an "operation of God."

Now what actually happened at the moment you got saved? I want you to envision that spiritually you are on the operating table and you have a deadly disease called sin. It has to be removed or else you will die. As you lay there on the table, in walks God the Father and God the Son.

An Operation of God

Just as a person has to sign release papers giving the doctors and the hospital permission to perform the surgery, you also have to give God permission to perform this spiritual operation. You do that by freely admitting you are sinner and you need a Savior. You believe Jesus Christ is your Savior, and what He did on the Cross is the only thing that can save you. When you, by faith, believe this and, by an act of your own free will, invite Jesus into your heart, you then have signed God's release papers. Oh hallelujah!

He first "circumcises" your heart. What does that mean? It means He cuts away the sinful part of your spiritual core, which is your sin nature. The sin nature is the part of man that rebels against God. It's that monster that lives within all of us. The sin nature was not earned by man; it was inherited by man through the seed of Adam.

When Adam and Eve disobeyed God in the Garden of Eden, the Bible says *"the eyes of them both were opened, and they knew that they were naked"* (Genesis 3:7). Before the fall, their eyes were closed to fleshly things. They walked in the Garden of Eden with God and there was no sin of lust or greed or any other foul thing in their minds. They were perfect. They had a human nature (Genesis 1:26-27) and they had a God consciousness, but they did not have a sin consciousness or a sin nature. However, the moment they disobeyed God and ate the forbidden fruit, the sin nature entered into their hearts.

In the operation room of God, the Lord first cuts away the sin nature. However, he does not remove it, interestingly enough. He simply detaches it, in essence, dethrones it. This is why the believer in Christ still continues to sin. However, the believer should not practice sin or be controlled by sin because, due to the spiritual operation of God, the sin nature has been detached. Sin has lost its control, and, therefore, the new believer can experience victory over sin.

A warning should be pointed out here. If that same believer doesn't understand how to live for God or how the Holy Spirit works, then the sin nature can reattach itself to the human nature. The sin nature can once again take over and become a problem. (This is discussed in great detail in my book *CrossEyed.*)

When the Lord "cuts away" or circumcises the sin nature, He then places, in the new believer's heart, some new machinery. He brings in the "Divine Nature." II Peter 1:4 states, *"Whereby are given unto us exceeding great and precious promises: that by these ye might be partakers of the divine nature, having escaped the corruption that is in the world through lust."*

The Divine Nature, or God's Nature, is His Holy Spirit, who comes into the heart of man to live. This implantation is what will give the believing sinner the assurance that he has been saved. He begins to experience a change immediately, whereby his love for God will deepen and his hatred for sin will increase. The amazing work of the Divine Nature, the Holy Spirit planted in the spiritual core of the believing sinner, is the greatest miracle ever performed on man.

The sin nature is cut away and the Divine Nature is implanted. This allows the believing sinner to overcome the lust of the flesh, the lust of the eyes, and the pride of life – the three main areas in which Satan tries to destroy man (I John 2:16).

Notice what Paul said in Colossians 2:11, *"In whom also ye are circumcised with the circumcision made without hands, in putting off the body of the sins of the flesh by the circumcision of Christ."*

Under the Old Testament, the Jewish boys – on the 8th day of life – would be circumcised, which was an outward sign that they belonged to God. Under the New Testament, circumcision is of the heart.

There is more to this operation with God. We are also, spiritually speaking, placed on the Cross and crucified with Jesus. Paul said, *"I am crucified with Christ"* (Gal. 2:20). We are baptized into His death. The scriptures say, *"Know ye not, that so many of us as were baptized into his death?"* (Romans 6:3).

What does it mean to be "baptized into His death?" The word "baptized" in the Greek is "baptizo." It is a word that is used for a ship that is sunk at sea, and when the water fills the ship it is submerged completely. At that moment, it is said that the ship is "baptizo" or in other words has been "completely sunk."

The word baptizo comes from the Greek word "bapto" which means "to dip or immerse, or to overwhelm, saturate, or baptize." So, when using the phrase "baptized into His death," he is saying, spiritually speaking, the believing sinner has been immersed into the death of Christ on the Cross. In other words, when Christ died, you, as a believer, died to self and surrendered all as well.

This is so important for the believer to understand because when you do, you will begin to understand how to have continual victory over sin. A dead man can't sin, he's dead. A dead man can't lust because he's dead.

If the believer doesn't know how to "walk in newness of life," or if he moves away from the Cross, the sin nature will reattach quickly. Regrettably, this happens to many new believers because they don't "know" (or haven't been taught) how to live the Christian life. Paul said *"know ye not,"* or "don't you know" (Romans 6:3).

So, the believer has been spiritually "dipped" into the death of Christ. But it doesn't stop there. He has also been *"buried with Christ"* (Col. 2:12). This means that when Jesus was put into the tomb, the believing sinner was placed in that tomb as well.

Buried with Christ

On my first trip to Israel, we visited the empty tomb where they believe Jesus was buried. Our guide took us into a cave cut into a hill, as that was the custom of burial sites of Jesus' day - they didn't bury people in the ground, but rather in caves. This particular cave, where Jesus was buried, had been purchased by a wealthy man by the name of Joseph of Arimathaea (Matt. 27:57-60).

As we entered the tomb, where tens of thousands, no doubt, have visited, I thought, what will I experience when I go in there? Will I sense the Holy Spirit in this place? I mean, this is the place where Jesus Christ rose from the dead! As I went in, the tour guide began to explain something that I didn't totally comprehend at the time. It would be some time later that the Lord would bring revelation to my heart.

The tour guide pointed to the place where they believe the body of Jesus was laid. You could see that it had been dug out of the rock. By measuring its length, they have estimated that Jesus could have been about 6'0 feet tall.

Our attention was next directed to the space on the opposite side of the cave which had not been prepared. This tomb had only been used for one body, the body of Jesus. However, there was room for another body. This struck me hard. I felt as though God was trying to show me something, but I could not discern at the time what it was.

Some weeks later, the Lord would show me the spiritual truth of this. I was taking a class in Baton Rouge, Louisiana at World Evangelism Bible College and my good friend, Bob Cornell, was teaching (whom I had traveled with to Israel, ironically enough). Bob was teaching on Romans 6:5 which says, *"For if we have been planted together in the likeness of his death, we shall be also in the likeness of his resurrection."*

Bob broke down these words "planted together." In the Greek it is the word "sumphutos" and it means "to grow along with." Brother Cornell pointed out that when you place a seed in the ground to grow a plant, you dig a hole and you plant one seed and that one seed, when watered and given sunlight, produces a crop.

He said when Christ was put into the tomb, the believing sinner was laid alongside Him (spiritually speaking). It was "two seeds in the same hole" – the perfect man, sinless Christ, and the sinner. But on that Sunday morning, when Christ was raised from the dead, only one came out – the resurrected Christ.

As a believer in Christ, you must see your old sinful self as being crucified with Christ and buried with Him, never to come out of that grave again. See the new man, the new you, born again with the Spirit living in you, now coming forth in Christ.

You need to see yourself "in Christ." Paul used this term over 170 times in the New Testament. What does it mean to be "in Christ"? We usually only think of Christ being in us, and that is true, but a better way to say it - the scriptural way - is to say that we are "in Christ."

We say we accepted Christ into our life, or, in other words, we chose Christ, but Jesus said, *"Ye have not chosen me, but I have chosen you"* (John 15:16).

Being "in Christ" was explained by the apostle Paul in Galatians 2:20, which says, *"I am crucified with Christ: nevertheless I live; yet not I, but Christ liveth in me: and the life which I now live in the flesh I live by the faith of the Son of God, who loved me, and gave himself for me."* It is now Christ whom I live for, not myself. I am now dead and hidden in Christ (Col 3:3).

Most of the preaching today over television and most Christian books are about self and self-promotion, which has caused great deception in the Church. The Christian life is not about "self," it is about Christ.

The spiritual surgery performed on you at salvation has buried that old man (your sinful self), as Paul wrote, *"Knowing this, that our old man is crucified with him, that the body of sin might be destroyed (this is speaking of the sin nature rendered idled), that henceforth we should not serve sin"* (Romans 6:6).

Notice the terminology *"we should not serve sin."* The word "serve" means to be in bondage. So many Christians find themselves in this position because they do not understand what it means to be "in Christ," and they don't know, nor understand, the operation that was performed on them at the moment of salvation.

It's like the man who has heart surgery and the doctors help remove the problem by opening arteries and getting the aortic valve to function properly. After surgery, the physicians are going to have strict guidelines and restrictions for this patient. If the person fails to follow those instructions, it won't be too long before he will have problems again.

Before this operation of God took place in the believing sinner's life, he was spiritually a mess. Notice what Paul said about his condition, *"And you, being dead in your sins and the uncircumcision of your flesh"* (Col.2:13). Before Christ, a person is "dead in sin." This means he is spiritually dead and on his way to eternal hell. Man just doesn't understand the seriousness of being in a non-Christian state. It is a very scary thing for any person to live without God. If he should die suddenly, he will go immediately to the place of eternal torment in hell (Luke 16:24).

But what is the key that unlocks the door and gives us access to God? What is it that causes God to do a spiritual operation on the heart of the sinner? Colossians 2:12 tells us that it is all *"through the faith."* Notice Paul used the definite article "the" before the word "faith," which means there is only one faith that God accepts. It is simply faith in *"Jesus Christ and Him crucified"* (I Cor. 2:2).

When faith is exercised, by the believing sinner, in what Christ did on the Cross, and he believes it to be the finished work (John 19:30) for salvation, then God, by His Spirit, begins to perform the spiritual operation that is needed to save the sinner and set him free from the bondage of sin.

The moment a person puts his faith in Christ and what Christ did at the Cross, then God the Father blots out (erases) the handwritten ordinances against him. The records of his sin and the commandments he has broken are no more. Jesus took them out of the way so that they could not keep us from experiencing a relationship with a Holy God and going to heaven. He nailed those accusations, that were against us, to His cross (Colossians 2:14).

He spoiled (ruined) principalities and powers (wicked powers) and openly made a show (demonstration of defeat) of them, triumphing over them (Col. 2:15). Where did He do that? At the Cross!

The greatest gift ever given to the believer is the Holy Spirit, and it was the work of the Cross that made all this possible. Before the Cross of Christ, people were held as servants, or slaves, under the law, but now, under grace, the sin debt has been paid - the law has been fulfilled. We can now become sons instead of servants (Gal. 4:5).

Now under grace, we are recipients of the promise, as Paul said, *"And if ye be Christ's, then are ye Abraham's seed, and heirs according to the promise"* (Gal. 3:29).

What is the Promise that Paul is speaking about? It is the Holy Spirit, which is only the first fruits of all the blessings that are waiting for us in heaven (Romans 8:23). The Bible tells in Acts 2:33, *"Therefore being by the right hand of God exalted and having received of the Father the promise of the Holy Ghost, he hath shed forth this, which ye now see and hear."*

What did they see and hear in the early church? They saw the people on fire for God and they heard them speaking in other tongues. The Holy Spirit, the Promise of the Father, was poured out at Pentecost.

Salvation is the greatest gift ever given to the world and the Baptism with the Holy Spirit is the greatest gift ever given to the Church. We ought to thank God everyday for this gift, as all the saints of the Old Testament lived and died without seeing the Promise come into their hearts and lives. *"And these all, having obtained a good report through faith, received not the promise (Christ and the Spirit of Christ, the Holy Spirit): God having provided some better thing for us, that they without us should not be made perfect"* (Heb. 11:39-40). Now, let's look at who the Holy Spirit is and what, exactly, He does in a believer's life.

Chapter 3

WHO IS THE HOLY SPIRIT AND WHAT IS HIS FUNCTION?

After experiencing the new birth, I began to read and study my Bible. I was so hungry to learn about Jesus, who He was and how He worked. I had very little, if any, knowledge regarding the Holy Spirit. I was a babe in Christ. But one thing I knew for sure: something had changed in my life. I heard a song one time, its lyrics were, "I'm born again, just like Jesus said. There's really been a change in me, born again, just like Jesus said."

But now I needed to learn who the Holy Spirit was and how He wanted to work in my life. One of the first things I learned about the Holy Spirit was how misunderstood He was and how easily He could be misrepresented. Thus began my journey of studying the scriptures regarding the third Person of the Trinity.

Who is the Holy Spirit?

A proper understanding of the person of the Holy Spirit is absolutely essential for every believer if we are to be the Christian God has created us to be. So, in our study let's lay a firm scriptural foundation for who the Holy Spirit is. First, let's look at who He is not. The Holy Spirit is not an "it." He is not a material substance, force or energy of nature. He is not some fuzzy, abstract thing and He is not some life-giving force.

The Holy Spirit is a Person! He thinks, He acts, He feels, He loves, He speaks, He guides, He directs, and He comforts. The Holy Spirit exhibits all the responses and qualities that identify one as a "person." He cannot be seen with the natural eye, but His actions fulfill all the requirements of a personality.

The Holy Spirit is God

The Holy Spirit is God - He is a distinct Person in the Triune Godhead. Christianity is not a polytheistic faith. Polytheism is the belief in and/or worship of multiple deities. Christianity teaches there is One God, represented in three persons. We refer to this triune God as the Trinity: God the Father, God the Son and God the Holy Spirit. Often, scripture refers to the Holy Spirit as the Holy Ghost, they are one and the same.

The scripture gives us evidence that the Holy Spirit is as much God as God the Father and God the Son. In other words, they are equal with one another. In the early church, Ananias and Sapphira sold a piece of land and said that the funds were intended to be used for the Church's needs. They then lied and held back a portion of the funds for personal means. Peter confronted them on their sin and said: *"Ananias, why hath Satan filled thine heart to lie to the Holy Ghost, and to keep back part of the price of the land?"* (Acts 5:3). He than went on to say, *"Thou hast not lied unto men, but unto God"* (Acts 5:4). This is a direct confession that the Holy Spirit is God.

In the Great Commission Jesus said, *"Go ye therefore, and teach all nations, baptizing them in the name of the Father, and of the Son, and of the Holy Ghost"* (Matthew 28:19). This is a direct reference by Jesus giving the Spirit equal authority with the Father and the Son. If the Holy Spirit was not God, this would be blasphemy.

Many times in scripture we will see the Trinity represented. At the baptism of Jesus we see God the Son, Jesus going into the waters as He is baptized by John. God the Father is heard saying from the heavens, *"This is my beloved Son, in whom I am well pleased."* We see the Spirit of God (the Holy Spirit) descending like a dove and coming upon Jesus (Matthew 3:13-17).

The scriptures say *"For there are three that bear record in heaven, the Father, the Word* (which is Jesus as we see in John 1:1-4, 14), *and the Holy Ghost: and these three are one"* (I John 5:7). The Holy Spirit is co-equal, co-existent and all-powerful, as is God the Father and God the Son.

The Holy Spirit is Indivisible

God's Spirit is indivisible, meaning you cannot divide or separate Him. He is one Spirit (Eph. 4:4-6). However, John, in the Book of Revelation speaks of the seven Spirits of God (Rev. 1:4, 3:1, 4:5 and 5:6).

John was caught up in a vision and saw heaven, the Throne, God, Jesus Christ, and the Holy Spirit. John also saw the Elders, the Angels, and events that were to take place in the future. And during all this he refers to the Spirits of God. The word "Spirit" is capitalized, meaning the Holy Spirit. The number seven is not to confuse us. The number "seven" in the Bible means "completion" or "perfection." Seven is said to be God's number, thus seven days in a week, which was set-up by God Himself. So, that doesn't mean that John saw seven Holy Spirits, but that he saw the completeness or the perfection of the Holy Spirit. The seven Spirits speak of the seven-fold working of the Holy Spirit which is found in Isaiah 11:2:

"And the spirit of the Lord shall rest upon him, the spirit of wisdom and understanding, the spirit of counsel and might, the spirit of knowledge and of the fear of the Lord."

There is one Holy Spirit but there are seven attributes of the Holy Spirit. They are:

1) Spirit of the Lord - God working in Spirit form.

2) The Spirit of Wisdom - The Holy Spirit is all wise.

3) The Spirit of Understanding - The Holy Spirit is the one who gives understanding in all things.

4) The Spirit of Counsel - He is the Ultimate Counselor.

5) The Spirit of Might - The Holy Spirit is all powerful.

6) The Spirit of Knowledge - The Holy Spirit is all knowing.

7) The Spirit of the Fear of the Lord - The Holy Spirit is the one who brings reverence for His name.

The Holy Spirit is United but Distinct

The Holy Spirit is one third of the Trinity and He is united with God the Father and God the Son in perfect unity, but also the Holy Spirit is distinct. God the Father, Son and Holy Spirit all have one purpose, one design and one desire. They are One in fulfillment of the duties pertaining to the Godhead, yet there are certain statements that can be made for each that don't apply for all. Jesus is the Son of the Father, He is not Father of the Son. The Holy Spirit proceeds from the Father and the Son, the Father and Son do not proceed from the Holy Spirit. Jesus sits at the right hand of the Father, the Father does not sit at the right hand of the Son.

In referring to the Holy Spirit, Jesus Himself said that if you commit the sin of blasphemy against the Holy Spirit, it will not be forgiven (Mark 3:29). The Holy Spirit is now present upon this earth, while God the Father and Jesus are in Heaven. We know that there is an omnipresent factor in the locations of the three members of the Trinity, but still these specific differences should be noted.

The Holy Spirit is Omnipresent

What does it mean that the Holy Spirit is omnipresent? This means that He is present everywhere at once (Psalm 139:7- 10). It is impossible to escape the presence of the Spirit of God, for He is everywhere. A sinner can attempt to run from God, but he can never escape the presence of God. You can either face Jesus as Savior in this world or you can face Him as Judge in the next world. Either way you will face Him; He is inescapable.

The Holy Spirit is Eternal

He had no beginning and He has no end. When God created man He said, *"Let us make man in our image, after our likeness"* (Genesis 1:26). One has to ask the question who is "us" and who is "our?" Obviously, this is referring to the Trinity.

The Holy Spirit is Omniscient

This means that the Holy Spirit is all-knowing and all-wise. His wisdom cannot be increased because He already knows all things (Isaiah 40:12-14). The Holy Spirit is the Teacher, He is perfect in knowledge and understanding (I Cor. 2:10-11).

The Holy Spirit is Omnipotent

This means the Holy Spirit is all-powerful. It is impossible for Him to be more powerful. In Micah 2:7 the question is asked, *"is the spirit of the Lord straitened?"* The word "straitened" means "narrowed." It suggests being limited or restricted. The answer to that question is obviously "no!" He is referred to as *"the power of the Highest"* (Luke 1:35). It is God's desire that every believer taps into His power (Acts 1:8).

The Names of the Holy Spirit

In Biblical times, names were very important because a person's name had special and unique meaning. The Lord could have called His Spirit anything He wanted to but He called His Spirit "Holy." One of His main functions is to make us "holy."

He is the one and only who sanctifies and purifies the believer. But the Holy Spirit is called by other names in Scripture. As we learn these names, we learn more about who the Spirit is and what He does. Here is a listing of some of His names:

- THE SPIRIT OF GOD (I Cor. 3:16, II Cor. 3:3)

- THE SPIRIT OF HIS SON (Rom. 8:9, Gal. 4:6, Phil.1:19)

- THE SPIRIT OF JUDGMENT (Isaiah 4:4, Isaiah 28:6, John 16:8)

- THE SPIRIT OF GRACE AND SUPPLICATIONS (Zech. 12:10)

- THE SPIRIT OF WISDOM AND KNOWLEDGE (Exodus 28:3, Deu. 34:9, Eph.1:17)

- THE SPIRIT OF COUNSEL (Isaiah 11:2)

- THE SPIRIT OF THE FATHER (Matt. 10:20)

- THE SPIRIT OF TRUTH (Eph. 6:17, II Tim. 3:16, John 14:16-17, 15:26, 16:13)

- THE SPIRIT OF HOLINESS (Romans 1:4, Lev. 19:2)

- THE SPIRIT OF LIFE (Romans 8:2. II Cor. 3:6)

- THE SPIRIT OF ADOPTION (Romans 8:15)

- THE SPIRIT OF PROMISE (Acts 2:1-4, 2:33, Joel 2:28, Eph. 1:13, Romans 8:16-17)

- THE SPIRIT OF HIS MOUTH (II Thes. 2:8, Heb. 4:12)

- THE SPIRIT OF FAITH (Romans 1:17, II Cor. 4:13)

- THE SPIRIT OF GLORY AND OF GOD (I Peter 4:14)

- THE COMFORTER (John 14:16)

How awesome is this third Person of the Trinity and how vast are His workings!

Symbols of the Holy Spirit

When learning about the Holy Spirit it is helpful to look at the symbols used in scripture to refer to Him. There are five symbols that are prominent in the Word of God to describe Him or to explain His work.

Water

Jesus used the term "Living Waters" to describe the Holy Spirit in the life of a believer. He said, *"He that believeth on me, as the scripture hath said, out of his belly shall flow rivers of living water"* (John 7:38). Notice the key to releasing this Living Water (which is the Holy Spirit) is to believe on Jesus and all that Jesus did at the Cross to make the Holy Spirit available to the believer.

When the fullness of the Holy Spirit is within us, there will be a flow of His Spirit out of us that will touch and refresh others. When the Word of God flows in a service, the anointing of the Holy Spirit can be like a "mighty river." The Holy Spirit is likened to living waters or a flowing river. He is like a spiritual Niagara Falls!

When you think of water and the purpose of it, you learn some things regarding the Holy Spirit. Physical water is needed to live and without water, in a few days, we will die. Spiritually speaking, we need the Holy Spirit in our lives or we will die. The only people who enter the Kingdom of God are those who are *"born of the Spirit"* (John 3:5). So, the Holy Spirit is the one who brings life to the soul, Eternal Life, such is the term used by Jesus "Living Water."

When the Samaritan woman at the well at Sychar came to draw water, Jesus was there and said to her, *"Give me to drink."* (John 4:7) This request by Jesus shocked the woman due to the fact that, in the culture of that day, Jews would not have any dealings with Samaritans, much less a Jewish *man* speaking to a Samaritan *woman*. The Samaritans were considered by the Jews to be rebels and unclean due to their mixture of Judaism and idolatry. But Jesus came to break the cultural barriers and He was reaching out to this woman to save her.

When the woman questioned why Jesus, being a Jew, would speak to a Samaritan, Jesus said, *"If thou knewest the gift of God, and who it is that saith to thee, Give me to drink; thou wouldest have asked of him, and he would given thee living water"* (John 4:10).

The woman did not understand that Jesus was speaking spiritually and she questioned Him on where this living water was of which He spoke. Jesus answered her and said: *"Whosoever drinketh of this water* (natural water) *shall thirst again: But whosoever drinketh of the water that I shall give him shall never thirst; but the water that I shall give him shall be in him a well of water springing up into everlasting life"* (John 4:13 -14).

In this passage we learn some important truths about the Holy Spirit. He is the one, and the only one, who can quench the thirst of man's soul. Nothing else in this world can satisfy, only the presence of God through His Holy Spirit.

When the Holy Spirit comes into your life, He fills a well deep down in your soul and you begin to live spiritually. The Greek word for life is "zoe" and it means spiritual energy or vitality. It simply means "a living organism." Christians should be the most alive people in the world. When we walk into a room the climate in that room should come alive. Any church that is dead and lifeless is not a true representation of Christ's Church. The Book of Acts Church was alive and miracles took place as the River of the Holy Spirit was flowing.

Oil

Another symbol used in the Bible to depict the Holy Spirit is oil. There are numerous uses of oil in the Old Testament which give more insight as to the workings of the Holy Spirit. Oil was used in the Old Testament to produce fuel for the lamps (Exodus 27:20), it was used for cooking (II Kings 4:1-7), it was used to consecrate the Priests to their offices (Ex. 29:7, 29-30, Lev. 8), it was used to anoint a King for Israel (I Samuel 10:1), and it was used in the New Testament to anoint people who asked to be healed (Mark 6:13).

We learn much about the Holy Spirit's activity from the symbol of oil. He provides power, energy and strength to the believer's life (Zech. 4:6); He anoints men in order to perform spiritual functions for Him (John 15:5. Phil 4:13). The oil symbolizes divine help to the one who is anointed and it represents the power of God as the Holy Spirit heals according to faith (James 5:14-15).

Stay Empty

There is a story in II Kings chapter four about a woman who came to the Prophet Elisha and cried over the death of her husband, who was a servant of the prophet. She said to Elisha, *"Thy servant my husband is dead; and thou knowest that thy servant did fear the Lord: and the creditor is come to take unto him my two sons to be bondmen"* (II Kings 4:1).

This woman was obviously in trouble because she was now a widow and her provider, her husband, was gone. She had no way to provide for her family's needs. Her creditors wanted to take her two sons and use them as servants in exchange for the debt she owed. Imagine the heartache and desperation this woman felt. Elisha asked her what she had left and the woman told him that she had nothing but one pot of oil.

Now, as they say, "little is much when God is in it." You may be someone who doesn't have a lot of money. You may think you don't have a lot of talent. There may not be much in your house, but let me tell you something, if you have the Holy

Spirit living in your house (your heart) you have everything you need. The pot of oil in the widow's house (II Kings 4:2) represents the Holy Spirit living in your house (i.e. your heart, I Cor. 3:16).

The Prophet Elisha told the woman to go and fetch as many empty jars as she could find from her neighbors and he said when she had done this to shut her door and start pouring the oil she had into the empty jars.

She did as the prophet said. When the empty jars were lined up, she began to pour the oil. The miracle happened; the oil started to multiply and the Bible says, *"And it came to pass, when the vessels were full, that she said unto her son, Bring me yet a vessel. And he said unto her, There is not a vessel more. And the oil stayed"* (II Kings 4:6)

There are some truths here that God wants to show us. First, you have to be empty to receive the infilling of the Holy Spirit (symbolized by the oil). Second, it takes faith to be filled with the Spirit. The woman had to believe what the Prophet told her was right even though it made no human sense to think that one jar of oil could fill so many. But the miracle of multiplication happened as she obeyed the words of the Prophet, which were really the Words of God. Thirdly, when there were no more empty vessels the miracle of multiplication ceased (stayed) and the oil stopped flowing. As long as we remain empty, the oil (Spirit) will continue to flow.

I remember when our youngest child, Emma, was born. My wife and I were not expecting to have any more children. We had three on earth (Andrew, Matthew and Hannah), and we had five in heaven. My wife had four miscarriages and one still birth and we both felt that it was time to stop trying to have more children.

Andrew, our oldest, and Hannah were born healthy, but our son Matthew suffers from a rare disorder called Glutaric Acidemia. This is a genetic disorder that has left him unable to walk, talk, hold his head up or eat on his own. The disorder is a hereditary disease. Neither my wife nor I have the disorder, however, our DNA is such that when matched together our genetic makeup can cause this disorder in our children. The doctors told us after Matthew was diagnosed that each succeeding child had a one out of four chance of contracting the disease.

So, when Hannah was born she was immediately tested and by the grace of God she tested negative. When Emma was born, she was tested and we felt confident that God would spare her as He did Hannah.

Three days after she was born, we received a call from the doctor that little Emma had tested positive and we needed to take her to Children's Hospital immediately for more testing. That call was the hardest call we had ever received in our lives. My mind raced as I thought about Emma's future; would she be in a wheel chair like her brother? When my wife hung up the phone after speaking with the doctor, I held her in my arms as we both cried together.

After taking her to the hospital, we returned home with Emma with strict instructions about her diet. Continual testing would be necessary. A few days later I walked into my den and all of sudden the Lord spoke to my heart. He actually spoke to me in the very same spot that my wife was standing when she took the call from the doctor telling her that Emma had tested positive for Glutaric Acidemia. It was as if God was saying, "The doctor gave you his diagnosis, but now I am going to give you mine."

He spoke just one word to me, He said, "Oil." I knew it was the Lord and I immediately asked, "Oil, what does that mean?" I asked the Lord if there was a scripture in the Bible to help me understand what He was saying to me. He instantly directed me to the story of the miracle of the widow's oil.

As I studied II Kings chapter four that day, the Lord showed me an incredible truth. He was saying to me that He is Emma's Healer and as long as I stayed empty and believed in Him for miracles, He would fill me continuously with His Holy Spirit and He would heal Emma.

At the writing of this book, Emma is almost six years old. To the Glory of God she is completely healthy and normal with no signs whatsoever of the terrible disease with which she was diagnosed at birth. God said "Oil" and He has been faithful to His Word in Emma's life. He is Emma's Healer! We named her Emma before we knew that she had this disorder. The name Emma actually means "Healer, or to be whole." Our God is an Awesome God! Remember, when you stay empty of self and the things of this world, His oil will flow in your life!

Dove

Another symbol of the Holy Spirit is the dove. The dove (or the form of the dove) is seen descending upon Jesus after He was baptized by John (Luke 3:22). There are several characteristics of a dove that give us insight into the Holy Spirit. The dove is one of God's most gentle creations and is a symbol of the love of God for His Chosen people. Doves are white and they speak of purity and were used in sacrificial offerings for purification at the Temple in Jerusalem. The dove is a symbol of peace and is often seen as a messenger. In Noah's day he sent a dove out to seek dry ground. If the dove didn't return then Noah would know the waters from the flood were receding.

The Holy Spirit functions in the believer's life as the One who is our peace, our source of gentleness and who brings the love of God into our lives. He assures us that we are the Children of God. The Bible says in Galatians 4:6: *"And because ye are sons, God hath sent forth the Spirit of his Son into your hearts, crying, Abba, Father."*

On one of our trips to Israel our tour guide pointed out an amazing thing. We were traveling by bus from the Town of Nazareth (where Jesus grew up) to the Sea of Galilee where

He began His earthly ministry. We drove by the Valley of the Doves. This is the path that the Messiah took when coming from Nazareth to the Sea of Galilee to begin His earthly ministry. How do we know He walked through this pathway? Because it is the only direct way to get to the Galilee from Nazareth.

The Sea of Galilee is one of the most peaceful and beautiful places in all of the world. It is surrounded by mountains. The Valley of the Doves gets its name from the fact that the doves can be seen daily flying through the valley. As we looked out our bus window I saw five doves flying through the valley even as she spoke. For the past 2,000 years it is as if these doves (symbolizing the Holy Spirit of God) are saying this is the pathway in which the Messiah walked.

Wind

Another symbol used in the Bible for the Holy Spirit is the wind. The contrast from the dove to the wind is amazing as the Holy Spirit is depicted as a *"rushing mighty wind"* (Acts 2:2). So, even though the Holy Spirit can be seen as peaceful and calm, He is also powerful and has the ability to move rapidly (like the wind on a stormy day).

As mentioned, I have been to Israel several times and each time we have taken a boat ride on the Sea of Galilee. I think it is a perfect place to learn about the Holy Spirit. On one of our boat trips, the Sea turned stormy very quickly and a beautiful day turned rainy and windy in a hurry. The fisherman told us that this is very common. One minute the Sea is calm and peaceful, and the next moment a storm of great proportion can be upon you. This fisherman told us that you have to respect the Sea of Galilee and so it is with the Holy Spirit. The Holy Spirit is as gentle as a Lamb, but He can also rage as a Lion. The symbol of the wind speaks of two main things: the Holy Spirit is powerful (He is "mighty") and He works like the wind.

The wind causes things to change. The wind causes things to move and move quickly if it is strong enough.

It has been said about God that He is a "go forward" God. I mean, two thirds of God's name is "Go!" He doesn't want you to stay in one place, He wants to move in your life in a way that you are constantly growing in Christ. In fact if you are not moving forward in your Christian walk, then you are going backwards. There is no such thing as staying neutral with God. Jesus said *"I know thy works, that thou are neither cold nor hot: I would thou wert cold or hot. So then because thou art lukewarm* (in the middle), *and neither cold nor hot, I will spue thee out of my mouth"* (Rev. 3:15-16).

The wind is invisible but the effects of the wind are very visible. Jesus, speaking of the born again experience said these words, *"The wind bloweth where it listeth, and thou hearest the sound thereof, but canst not tell whence it cometh, and whither it goeth: so is every one that is born of the Spirit"* (John 3:8).

You probably won't see the Holy Spirit come into your life when you are born again but you will see the change that He will make as a result of coming in. No man has ever seen the wind, but He has sure experienced the effects of the wind, so it is with the Spirit of God.

Fire

On the top of Mount Carmel, Elijah, the Prophet, called together all the false prophets of Baal. He told them to cry out to their god and ask him to send fire down upon the altar. Elijah said he would do the same and whoever sent the fire down, either their god or his God, would be the God that the people would worship (I Kings 18). The Bible says the false prophets of Baal attempted to call fire down but there was no answer and no manifestation. The false prophets, with all the people watching, grew desperate and the Bible says they even began to cut themselves in order to get their god (which was no god at all) to respond. But the heavens were silent.

Then Elijah stepped up and the Bible says he first repaired the altar of the Lord that had been broken down. He placed the bullock on the repaired altar, a type of Christ on the Cross. He poured water in the trench around the altar, a type of the Holy Spirit. He then called on the Lord and God Almighty responded. The God of Abraham, Isaac, and Jacob sent down holy fire and Elijah's sacrifice was consumed as well as the wood, stones, soil and water surrounding it. When all the people saw this great manifestation of the Lord, they began to shout, "*The Lord, he is the God; the Lord, he is the God*" (I Kings 18:39). In essence they were saying, "Elijah's God is God." Elijah then directed the people to kill all the false prophets of Baal.

The Bible says that our God is an all-consuming fire. The fire speaks of judgment and it also speaks of cleansing and righteousness. This is what the Holy Spirit has come to do in our lives (John 16:8).

The Holy Spirit has been given to mankind so that we can have a personal relationship with God. Without the Spirit a man cannot know God personally. He can know *about* God but he cannot know Him intimately. Remember in the Tabernacle and in the Temple, above the Ark of the Covenant, the glory of God (His presence) dwelt between the Cherubims and the Mercy Seat in the Holy of Holies. He now dwells in the hearts of born again believers who repent of their sins and put their faith in Christ and what Christ did at the Cross to remove their sins.

God the Holy Spirit is there in the hearts of the believers as the first fruits of their salvation (Romans 8:23), to bring them into relationship with Him and to give them victory over sin. The believer must remember that the Holy Spirit is only there because of what Jesus did on the Cross and the Holy Spirit moves and works through continued faith in Jesus Christ and Him crucified (Romans 8:2-3).

If the believer in Christ depends on anything other than Jesus Christ and the Cross, then the Spirit will be grieved and begin to be quenched, which means He will be hindered in helping that particular believer live for God.

When a person comes to Jesus Christ and is born again, at that moment, the divine nature is implanted into the believer's heart and life (II Peter 1:4). This new nature is the person of the Holy Spirit and He has come to give victory over sin and to bring us into a personal relationship with Jesus. When the divine nature is implanted into the heart of the believing sinner, the potential for supernatural things to occur is now present.

Chapter 4

THE FRUIT
OF THE HOLY SPIRIT

We receive the Holy Spirit when we come to faith in Christ and Him crucified. The Holy Spirit comes into the life of the believing sinner to equip, empower, and transform him into a person who reflects the nature and likeness of Jesus Christ.

The book of Galatians lists the nine fruit of the Holy Spirit (Gal. 5:22, 23). While the nine gifts of the Spirit are the manifestation of the Spirit working outwardly for ministry, the nine fruit of the Spirit are the manifestation of the Spirit working inwardly in the believer to produce holy characteristics.

At the moment of salvation, you put your faith in Jesus Christ as the source of salvation and the Cross as the means of salvation. This act of repentance and faith is what brought the Holy Spirit, the Spirit of Christ, into your life. At that moment, the inward work of the Holy Spirit was available to you.

While most of this book, *A Mighty River*, will speak about the outward working of the Holy Spirit, we must recognize the transformation that He desires to make from the inside out in each and every believer as well.

Spiritual Fruit

Jesus promised that He would give us abundant life. In John 10:10 He said, *"The thief cometh not, but for to steal, and to kill, and to destroy: I am come that they might have life, and that they might have it more abundantly."*

The good news of the Gospel is that, not only did Jesus come to save you from hell and give you eternal life with Him in Heaven, but He came also to give you abundant life here on this earth. We are not speaking of wealth, position, or power here, but the ability that comes from the Holy Spirit to walk in victory every day of your life. Don't misunderstand, this world is going to persecute the true believer in Christ, the Bible promises that (II Tim. 3:12). However, through faith in Jesus Christ, the Holy Spirit produces His fruit even in, and sometimes even more abundantly during, those times.

The Bible lists nine fruit of the Holy Spirit. These are not the fruit of man, nor his works, but the Bible calls them the "Fruit of the Spirit." The nine listed in Galatians 5:22, 23 are **Love, Joy, Peace, Longsuffering, Gentleness, Faith, Meekness, and Temperance**. The number nine in the Bible is the number of the Holy Spirit. These fruit are all produced only by, and through, the Holy Spirit operating in the believer's life.

Love (Charity)

The first fruit of the Spirit spoken of is "Love." The Greek word for "love" is "agape," not found in classical Greek, but only in revealed religion. In the Lexical aid, it is translated "charity" meaning "benevolent love." Its benevolence, however, is not shown by doing what the person loved desires but what the one who loves deems as needed by the one loved.[1]

The highest, deepest, widest love was shown at Calvary. John 3:16 says, *"For God so loved the world, that he gave his only begotten Son, that whosoever believeth in him should not perish, but have everlasting life."* God did not give according to what man wanted, but according to what man needed; the

Savior, Jesus Christ. For man to show love to God, he must first understand and appropriate God's agape, for only God has such an unselfish love.[2]

The natural man can love things and love people. God has given him that ability through the human nature. However, only the Divine Nature, given to man at the moment of salvation, can produce the "agape" kind of love, this most important fruit of the Spirit. God defines His love in I Corinthians 13. (Read those words and use them as a measuring rod in your own life for the love you offer and receive.)

God's love for man was demonstrated and man's love for God must be as well. True love always shows itself with action. If you say that you love someone then your lifestyle will reflect it. Jesus said, *"If ye keep my commandments, ye shall abide in my love"* (John 15:10). One's obedience proves one's beliefs. The Word of God says in James 2:17, *"Even so faith, if it hath not works, is dead, being alone."*

You can be a great, anointed preacher of the Gospel, you can be the best singer in the Church, operate in all of the gifts of the Spirit, have faith to move mountains, but if you do not have love, the Bible says you have nothing (I Cor. 13:1-2). We sing the words to a song that say, "they will know that we are Christians by our love." We love because He first loved us. The greatest display of love is found in the life of Christ. Jesus doesn't try to love, He is love! Our love for God and our love for others must be evident and shine through our lives, and this can only truly be produced by the Holy Spirit.

Joy

The second fruit of the Spirit listed is joy. In the Greek, this word is "chara" and it means "to rejoice." It means to show great exultation or exuberant joy for the Lord.[3] A Spirit-filled believer will be one who shows great joy for Jesus and wants to exalt His Name. The Holy Spirit didn't come to exalt Himself, but He came to exalt Jesus.

Joy comes from within and it never changes. You can be going through a hard time in this world, but your joy from, and for, Jesus is still there. The Bible says, *"For the joy of the Lord is your strength"* (Nehemiah 8:10). It didn't say my joy or your joy, but it said the *"joy of the Lord."* Our joy can be up and down, but His joy is always up. Heaven is always shouting and the angels are always singing. It is the Lord's joy and not our joy that is our strength. Christians should be the most joyful people in the whole world. We are the only people who really have something to shout about. We have the Holy Spirit in us and He is full of joy!

This joy from the Holy Spirit will lead those in the world to wonder, ask questions and some may even mock out of envy. The joy of the Spirit is very attractive to the world and gets its attention. On the Day of Pentecost, when the disciples were filled with the Spirit, the people were all amazed, but some were in doubt saying, *"What meaneth this? Others mocking said, These men are full of new wine"* (Acts 2:12, 13).

The Bible says that we are not to be drunk with wine, but are to be filled with the Spirit (Eph 5:18). The closest thing the world has to compare with being filled with the Holy Spirit is getting drunk on alcohol, which doesn't even come close. The world doesn't know that being filled with the Spirit is being filled with the joy of the Lord, and it doesn't have to wear off, but it can be with you all the time and without negative side effects. The Bible says, *"For the Kingdom of God is not meat and drink; but righteousness, and peace, and joy in the Holy Ghost"* (Romans 14:17).

Peace

The third fruit mentioned is peace. It has been said that God created the human heart with a God-shaped hole in it. What this means is that, no matter what the person tries to do or achieve, he will never have peace because only God can fill the empty void in the heart. The missing piece to the human puzzle is the "Peace of God." Jesus Christ is known as the "Prince of Peace." Only Christ, and what He did on the Cross, can bring peace into the heart of the sinner.

Placing our faith in Jesus Christ brings the peace of God to sinful man. The word "peace" in the Greek is "eirene" and means "rest." "It denotes a state of untroubled, undisturbed, well being. It refers to mercy for the consequences of sin. Peace as a Messianic blessing is that state brought about by the grace and loving mind of God wherein the derangement and distress of life caused by sin are removed. Hence the message of salvation is called the Gospel of Peace."[4]

Jesus gave the ultimate invitation when He said, *"Come unto me, all ye that labour and are heavy laden, and I will give you rest. Take my yoke upon you, and learn of me; for I am meek and lowly in heart: and ye shall find rest unto your souls. For my yoke is easy, and my burden is light"* (Matthew 11:28-30). There is a world seeking and longing for peace of heart, but missing the One who brings it, our Triune God!

Longsuffering (Patience)

The Bible says, *"My Brethren, count it all joy when ye fall into divers temptations; Knowing this, that the trying of your faith worketh patience"* (James 1:2-3). The fruit of "Longsuffering" (patience), as with all the fruit of the Spirit, takes time to develop (or ripen) in our life. It is through trials and tribulations that patience is developed. The word "longsuffering" means "forbearance, to endure suffering with patience."

Many great men and women of God have suffered through some of the most trying experiences in life. But when they have overcome the trial, they are more able to handle the next situation with greater patience and faith in what the Lord can, and will, do in the midst of adversity. Great faith must be tested greatly.

Gentleness (Kindness)

The word "gentleness" is "chrestotes" in the Greek and it means "kindness." It implies the harmlessness of the dove.[5] The dove is seen to be the most gentle creature that God ever created and is one of the symbols used in the Bible for the Holy Spirit. One who is filled with the Holy Spirit will exhibit the characteristic of having a spirit that is kind and gentle. These two characteristics will draw people.

Jesus was kind as He fed the 5,000 with the loaves and fish. As well, He was gentle as He held the small children in His arms. The world is accustomed to harsh and cold treatment, not kindness and gentleness. The fruit of gentleness follows the example of Jesus Christ. He was never harsh, but He always appreciated and respected others. He seeks to heal and unite.[6]

Goodness

Another fruit of the Holy Spirit is goodness. The word for "goodness" in the Greek is "agathosune" and it means "active goodness." It is a characteristic that is energized, expressing itself in active good.[7] Many will say, when speaking of a certain Christian, "He is a good man!" This simply means that he doesn't just talk the talk, but he walks the walk. This fruit of the Spirit produces a person who helps others in need.

In the parable of the Good Samaritan, we see goodness manifested as a certain man from Jerusalem was on his way to Jericho. He was attacked by thieves along the way who beat him and robbed him of all his money. They left him in the road to die, as he was badly wounded. Jesus said there were two men who saw him and passed by without helping him, one was a Priest and the other man was a Levite - two religious men, but neither of them stopped.

The Good Samaritan not only ministered to the wounds of the injured man, but he took him to the inn and paid for all of his expenses until he regained his strength. The Gospel of Jesus Christ is not only a "tell me" Gospel, but it is also a "show me" Gospel. It is true that the world does not care how much you know until they first know how much you care.

This goodness is a fruit in the life of the Christian who is walking with the Lord. It must never be confused with or seen as an entrance fee or way into heaven. We have said, and will say once again, that faith in Jesus Christ as the Son of God and believing in Him and His sacrifice on the Cross of Calvary is the only way anyone will get into heaven. No matter how good we are, or how many good deeds we have done, they will never be enough to pay the price for eternal life.

Faith (Faithfulness)

The fruit of faithfulness is so important. It demonstrates to the world that Christians live a life trusting in God, regardless of the circumstances. The Holy Spirit grows this fruit in the life of a believer over time, as He does all the fruit. The world sees this quality in a Christian and marvels at how he can stay so committed to Christ, but it is really the Spirit who continues to build faith in the believer as he grows in Christ. In good times and in bad *"we walk by faith and not by sight"* (II Corinthians 5:7). We walk with faces set like flint toward the victory of Calvary. In it, and through it, God receives all the glory.

Those early years, when I first got saved, were not easy. The loneliness of losing all my friends and the persecution was difficult, but the Holy Spirit was producing in me the fruit of faithfulness and showing me that God blesses faithfulness.

The Bible says, *"And let us not be weary in well doing: for in due season we shall reap, if we faint not"* (Galatians 6:9).

Meekness

The fruit of meekness is a quality that flows from a humble heart that has been touched and changed by the Holy Spirit. This fruit is a humble concern for the welfare of others. It is not self-centered or self-righteous, but walks in thankfulness of God's grace. Meekness never demands its own way, and it is not manipulative. It is not quarrelsome, nor does it seek to defend itself. It courageously stands for truth, but does not force its will upon another.

The fruit of meekness disarms the world to the point that it doesn't really know what to do with this quality. The opposite of meekness is a brass, boisterous and loud spirit. The person who lacks meekness is, many times, condescending, has to win every argument and tries to make others feel inferior.

Someone who is meek, however, is someone who has an inner confidence carried within him, and a humbleness that says everyone else is more important than he is. The Proverb says, *"A soft answer turns away wrath: but grievous* (harsh) *words stir up anger"* (Prov. 15:1). The meek know how to disarm the world and leave it speechless.

Jesus said, in the Sermon on the Mount, *"Blessed are the meek: for they shall inherit the earth"* (Matt. 5:5). Meekness must never be confused with weakness. The only personal words that Jesus ever used to describe Himself were, *"For I am meek and lowly in heart"* (Matthew 11:29). He is the greatest model of meekness operating in its fullness in a human being.

Temperance (Self Control)

The last fruit of the Holy Spirit listed in Galatians 5:22, 23, is one of the most important and necessary: self control. This fruit, when exhibited, will demonstrate to a lost world the power of the Holy Spirit to give victory over sinful temptation.

Paul said, *"And they that are Christ's have crucified the flesh with the affections and lusts"* (Galatians 5:24). Self control means that one is able to overcome temptation to commit immorality, anger, gluttony, covetousness, etc., as these weaknesses of the flesh are unable to overtake us and control our lives when this fruit is present and operating in us.

There are many Christians today who are ruining their witness for Christ because they lack self control. Many of them are born again and love God, but they are failing God because they cannot control the lust of their flesh. Without a proper understanding of how to walk in the Spirit they, instead, carry out the lusts of the flesh (Gal. 5:16).

The fruit of self control is produced by the Spirit, and not of the flesh, as it is with all of the fruit. The Holy Spirit will develop this fruit as one looks to the Cross for complete victory over sin. The Bible says, *"For sin shall not have dominion over you, for ye are not under law but under grace"* (Romans 6:14). When it says we are under grace, it means we are looking to the Cross for the victory over sin. Our dependence is on the Holy Spirit (Zech 4:6) to give us what we need to be strong and rise above temptation, and all of this is based on what Christ accomplished on Mount Calvary (Gal. 2:20, 21).

Final Words

At the moment of salvation, God places His Holy Spirit within every believer. With the indwelling of His Spirit comes the fruit of His Holy Spirit. As the believer seeks to change from the life he had according to the lusts of his flesh, he can now call upon the Spirit's help. He can now ask and depend upon God to begin to change him from the inside out. Through the power of the Holy Spirit operating in him, he can now begin to walk and exhibit all the fruit of the Spirit.

If you resist or limit the Holy Spirit's work in any way, you will not walk in the abundance that God intended you to have. You will not become the person God created you to be. You will not be the witness to family, friends and your world of the life changing power of Almighty God.

To invite and allow the Holy Spirit to have His way in your life will produce a person who will walk in the fullness of love, joy, peace, longsuffering, gentleness, goodness, faith, meekness and temperance. This person, although not perfect, will be sold out to and full of the Holy Spirit's fruit. May we each say daily, You are the potter, Lord, and I am the clay. Mold me and make me as You created me to be through the power of Your Holy Spirit for Your glory!

Chapter 5

THE HOLY SPIRIT
IN THE BOOK OF ACTS

The greatest thing in life is to know God. Knowing Him is a joy unspeakable and beyond description. We know God the Father through God the Son, and we experience God the Son through God the Holy Spirit. To know and understand more about the Father, Son and the Holy Spirit is life's greatest pursuit.

The Holy Spirit is the power source of the entire Christian experience, as everything God does is by His Spirit (Zech. 4:6). For the believer in Christ there can be no subject of more vital significance than the study of the Holy Spirit. The book of Acts has been written so we can learn the ways of the Spirit. It is one thing to learn the doctrine or the theology of the Holy Spirit and another to know Him by experience. The Book of Acts provides us with a history of how people did not just learn about the Holy Spirit, but actually experienced Him in their lives. My prayer is that you will not only learn about the Holy Spirit, but you will experience the Holy Spirit in your daily walk with God.

The Book of Acts was written by Luke, the physician, to Theophilus as a sequel to the Gospel that bares his name. The Gospel of Luke relates *"all that Jesus began both to do and teach"* (Acts 1:1). The Acts of the Apostles (or the Acts of the Holy Spirit), on the other hand, begins with the ascension of Jesus and tells the story of how the Gospel message was spread far beyond the confines of the Jewish community.

It is believed that Luke concluded his writing of the Book of Acts in A.D. 61. It is clear that Luke was with Paul on certain occasions and was an eye witness to the things he has written about. In fact, many believe it was Luke whom Paul referred to in II Cor. 8:18 when he said, *"And we have sent with him the brother, whose praise is in the gospel throughout all the churches."*

Luke's purpose in writing the Book of Acts was not to give a complete history of the growth of the early Church, but only to list those events with which he was familiar.

The Book of Acts Doesn't End, it Just Quits

The Book of Acts has no closing salutation as compared to other books (see Romans 16:27, I Cor. 16:24, II Cor. 13:14, Gal. 6:18, Eph. 6:24, Phil 4:23, Col. 4:18, etc.). One could, however, attempt to make a case that those writings were written by Paul and Luke's style of writing was different and he didn't use a closing salutation. Well, let's see if that is true. In Luke 24:53 we see the "Amen" but, in the Book of Acts, Luke didn't close his letter, he just stopped writing. Why is that significant? I believe the Lord was sending a message to all those skeptics who say that the working of the Holy Spirit ceased with the death of the Apostle John, at least as it relates to the gifts of the Spirit. God is saying that His Spirit is still working today. I believe the Book of Acts will continue until Jesus returns.

It Takes Faith to Fully Embrace the Holy Spirit

Those who make a case that the Holy Spirit is not working as He did in the first century Church, lack the faith to believe. A lack of faith in the Holy Spirit's power to do the same as He did in the Book of Acts is a sad reality of Church history.

There is a teaching called dispensationalism which teaches that God moves differently in different "dispensations." The Dispensation of Innocence is the time period from the creation of man to the fall of man. The Dispensation of Conscience is the time period from the fall of man to the giving of the Law on Mount Sinai. After the Law was given, the next period is known as the Dispensation of Law, which extended from the time of Moses to the time of Christ. When Jesus Christ died on Calvary, we entered into a time known as the Dispensation of Grace. We have been in this dispensation for almost 2,000 years, and when Jesus Christ comes back we will enter into the Dispensation of the Kingdom Age.

However, under the Dispensation of Grace, the Church age began on the Day of Pentecost and the power, in terms of the gifts of the Spirit, has not ceased. God did not turn off the power switch when the Apostle John died or when we received the Bible in full written form, as some teach. There is no Bible reference for such a belief. The Word of God states that *"Jesus Christ is the same yesterday and today and forever"* (Hebrews 13:8). In fact, the Bible warns against this limited faith and what it will do in the Church age if believed. Consider the following scriptures:

Those that deny the power we are to turn away from (II Tim. 3:1-5).

The gift of the Holy Spirit is for the entire church age and beyond (Acts 2:37-39).

Limited faith equals limited miracles seen (Mark 6:5-6).

The Bible says *"All things are possible to him who believeth."* There is no qualification of dispensation in these words of Jesus. "All" means all (Mark 9:23).

Jesus said these signs of the Holy Spirit will follow them that believe. So it only stands to reason that if we don't believe we won't see these signs in the church (Mark 16:15-18).

In historical revivals signs and wonders accompanied the move of God (Acts 2:1-4, 4:31, 10:44, 19:1-6).

The Holy Ghost in the Book of Acts

There are many things that the Holy Spirit is recorded doing in the Book of Acts. He has not changed today. He wants to be active in every church and in every believer and He will be active if that church or person, regardless of what denomination they may be, will only believe in His power. God spoke through Malachi the Prophet and said these words, *"For I am the Lord, I change not"* (Mal. 3:6a).

The Book of Acts is the Pattern

In the Book of Acts we see the great flow of the Holy Spirit and, as a result, <u>souls are saved, lives are changed, sick bodies are healed, believers are baptized in the Holy Spirit, demons are dispelled and the dead are raised</u>. It is filled with the actions of the Holy Spirit. The believer in Christ will do well to study the workings of the Holy Spirit in the Book of Acts, as it has been written to teach us how the Spirit of God acts in human endeavors. Be assured the Holy Spirit is still moving today as He moved in the Book of Acts. He will move in your life as He wills, if you will only invite and allow Him to.

The Holy Spirit gave the blueprints, in the Book of Acts, for what the Church should look like. As we study, it becomes apparent how far the Church has fallen and just how much we need a revival to bring us back to the original design. Jeremiah said, *"Thus saith the Lord, Stand ye in the ways, and see, and ask for the old paths, where is the good way, and walk therein, and ye shall find rest for your souls"* (Jeremiah 6:16). The modern Church keeps looking for new methods, but it is the "Old Paths" that we need.

Over 50 times the title or name "Holy Spirit," "Holy Ghost," "Spirit" or "Spirit of God" is used in the Book of Acts. Therefore, it is blatantly obvious that the Holy Spirit is the Principle Player in the early Church. He is paramount, predominant, probing, and powerful in everything that is done. There is no mistaking His identity and direction.

The Holy Spirit is actually the dynamo, the generator, the power source of the Godhead. The power of the Holy Spirit is an explosive power, a great mighty power, while at the same time a gentle power. The Holy Spirit's power is needed to overcome the power of darkness.

There are warnings in the Bible to not limit God's power. We are warned not to deny God's power (II Tim. 3:5), nor grieve His Spirit (Eph. 4:30), nor quench the Spirit (I Thess. 5:19), nor forbid the gifts of the Spirit (I Cor. 14:39) and not to oppose God's power, for if we do then we are "fighting against God" (Acts 5:38-39).

In the Book of Acts, we find powerful, anointed preaching and teaching of Jesus Christ crucified, buried and raised from the dead. Any church not making the Message of the Cross their main message is not following the pattern of the Book of Acts (Acts 5:42).

The early Church saw the sick being healed in the name of Jesus and miracles being performed. We find the oppressed being set free and demons cast out. We find believers being baptized in the Holy Spirit with the evidence of speaking with other tongues. We find the gifts of the Holy Spirit in operation. We find a fellowship of churches in one accord with a common purpose and with like doctrine. Prayer and fasting is a common occurrence and the Gospel is being spread abroad (world evangelism holds priority). This is the pattern that all churches must follow.

Some have claimed that the Book of Acts is not meant to serve in a doctrinal capacity. However, that is error. The Book of Acts is, in fact, doctrine carried out in actions, and it is a pattern which the Church is to follow. The blueprint for how to build a church or a youth ministry is found in the book of Acts. You don't need the latest strategy or program, you simply need to follow the pattern of the Holy Spirit in the Book of Acts.

Luke writes in Acts 1:1, *"The former treatise have I made, O Theophilus, of all that Jesus began both to do and teach,"* and it is a key verse that states that the Book of Luke was about the life of Christ - what He did and what He taught. This one statement sets the stage for the entirety of the Book of Acts, which now gives the continuation of Jesus' ministry lived out through the believers (Mark 16:15-20, John 14:12).

At the starting gate, Luke, inspired by the Holy Spirit, presents Jesus as the foundation and standard for all things done now in the Church. So, the Book of Acts is to serve as the pattern and model for what Jesus is doing now through His body, the Church.

Acts 1:2 says, *"Until the day in which he was taken up, after that he through the Holy Ghost had given commandments unto the apostles whom he had chosen."*

The phrase, *"after that he through the Holy Ghost,"* refers to the fact that the Holy Spirit is now the Speaker, Comforter, Helper, Teacher, Actor, etc. This tells us that everything that Jesus does on earth is done through the agency, office and ministry of the Holy Spirit.

Everything the believer does should be through the leadership and direction of the Holy Spirit. Therefore the believer must seek His direction for everything. <u>The prayer life of the believer is most important</u>.

What the Pattern is Not

What we don't find in the Book of Acts are religious denominations, religious hierarchy or churches filled with programs and without the presence of God. We do not find seeker sensitive churches. We don't find churches that only meet once a week for one hour services or churches that are completely accepted by the world. Instead we see a persecuted church, persecuted mainly by the religious institutions of that day.

We don't find empty or non-existent prayer meetings, but we find the Church praying and seeking daily and even meeting all night in prayer (Acts 2:42-47, 12:3-17).

Jesus' Last Words

Jesus could have talked about anything before He ascended, but He chose to speak on the Promise of the Father: the Baptism with the Holy Spirit. He commanded His disciples not to depart from Jerusalem, but *"wait for the promise of the Father"* (Acts 1:4).

The Baptism with the Holy Spirit was prophesied by John the Baptist and now the time had come, as Jesus ascended, for that ministry to begin. It began at Pentecost and has not ceased throughout this present age, despite what some have taught.

In Acts 1:8, Jesus said the Baptism with the Holy Spirit would give them "power" as well as prepare them to be "witnesses." The word "power" here in the Greek is "dunamis," meaning miraculous power.

A lot of believers interpret the word "witnesses" in Acts 1:8 to mean evangelism. Although it includes evangelism, it has a deeper meaning than that. The word "witness" here is "martus" and it means "one who remembers, one who has information or knowledge or joint-knowledge of anything; hence one who will give information, bring to light, or confirm anything." Thus a martus is one who announces and spreads the facts of the Gospel. They are ones who have "experiential knowledge." It is also used as a designation of those who have suffered death as the consequence of confessing Christ. Which means a martus is willing to even die if that is what it takes to get the Lord's message to a lost world.

Every believer must understand that the power of the Holy Spirit (i.e. Baptism with the Holy Spirit) is necessary to operate in "miraculous power" and to be a witness unto Jesus. The disciples (120 people) followed the command of Jesus and waited for the Promise of the Father, the Baptism with the Holy Spirit.

What the Church Did Before They Saw an Outpouring of the Holy Spirit

Again, the Book of Acts is our blueprint to teach us great truths about how the Holy Spirit works. The question that many ask today is what will it take to see another great move of God in our day? Here are a few clues we find from the early Church answering that question:

- They waited on God - tarried (Acts 1:4).

- They continued in prayer. Continual is "proskarteree" and means to endure, to tarry, remain somewhere; refers to those who insist on something or stay close to someone (Col. 4:2, Rom. 12:12, Acts 2;42, 6:4). The early Church went to all night prayer watches and fastings.

- There was supplication. This word is "deesis" which means a more general request made toward God in particular.

- They were in one accord. This means they had corporate unity among the brethren (Acts 2:1).

The word brethren ("adelphos" in the Greek) means a community of love based on the commonality of believers due to Christ's work. The only unity that God will recognize is the "Unity of the Spirit" (Eph. 4:3) which is a unity based on sound doctrine, particularly the Message of the Cross and the power of the Holy Spirit (I Cor. 1:18, 2:2-5, Romans 8:2-5).

The Outpouring of the Holy Spirit

The outpouring of the Holy Spirit, recorded in the Book of Acts, occurred on the Day of Pentecost. The Day of Pentecost is 50 days after the Feast of Passover (the word Pentecost means the 50th day after Passover). Passover commemorated the killing of the paschal lamb, with the placing of its blood on the doorposts in Egypt. The blood of the lamb protected the children of Israel during the tenth plague and caused the death angel to (which brought death to the firstborn) "pass over" them.

It was no coincidence that Jesus was offered as our Paschal Lamb on the commemoration of the original Passover. The killing of the paschal lamb was a type (the prophetic foreshadowing) of Jesus' later role as the Paschal Lamb for the world. The Jews today still celebrate the Passover as a historic occasion, not realizing its prophetic significance in regard to Jesus Christ.

Like the Feast of Passover, the Feast of Pentecost had special significance. It was the Feast of Weeks. This was the day when the celebrants considered God's bountiful blessings as they came from their land. Just as Pentecost came after Passover, so the Baptism with the Holy Spirit comes after Salvation.[1]

On the Day of Pentecost, God came suddenly, meaning "happening or coming unexpectedly." There was a sound from heaven as a rushing, mighty (forceful) wind (the word for wind is "pnoe" and means to breathe, blow, a violent wind, a tornado or violent storm).

The disciples were all filled with the Holy Spirit and began to speak with other tongues (different languages were given out) as the Spirit gave them utterance. The disciples did the speaking and the Holy Spirit gave the utterance.

There were people from every nation in Jerusalem at that time due to observing the celebration of the Feast of Weeks. Obviously, the Holy Spirit timed this perfectly so that the news of the outpouring of the Holy Spirit could spread faster and the power of God could be witnessed.

The First Sermon of the Church

On the Day of Pentecost, Peter gave the first sermon of the early Church. He was the one who had denied Christ three times just 50 days earlier. But he was the one that Jesus chose (Matt. 16:16-18). Peter declared that what the people were seeing and hearing was the beginning of the fulfillment of the prophecy given by the Prophet Joel (Joel 2:28-29). He said *"this is that which was spoken by the Prophet Joel"* (Acts 2:16).

The content of Peter's first sermon should be the main content of the message given during the Church age. Let's take a closer look at the first sermon of the Church age:

1) He preached Jesus of Nazareth, a man approved of God among you by miracles, wonders and signs. Jesus Christ is same today (Heb. 13:8)!

2) He preached on the Cross of Christ. He was crucified by the determined counsel and foreknowledge of God (Acts 2:23).

3) He preached on the resurrection of Christ - Peter said *"He has loosed the pains of death"* (Acts 2:24).

4) Peter said the Prophet David prophesied of the Christ (Acts 2:25-31). So, "this is that" not only was what the Prophet Joel had said, but was also based on the prophecy of David. Peter is saying "this is He." The eye witnesses of Jesus' resurrection were present on the Day of Pentecost to witness to the fact that Jesus Christ had risen (Acts 2:32).

5) Peter preached the Baptism with the Holy Spirit (Acts 2:33).

6) Peter closes his message by declaring that Jesus is both Lord and Christ and he is not afraid to point the finger at those who crucified the Messiah (Acts 2:34-36).

Peter, being filled with the Holy Spirit and anointed of God to preach, sees the conviction of God fall on the people. They were "pricked" (pierced thoroughly) in their heart. For man to be saved, the Gospel message must reach the heart. The word for "heart" is "kardia"- meaning the thoughts, reasoning, understanding, will, judgments, designs, love, hatred, fear, joy, sorrow, etc. When people are really ready to receive Christ, they will say, "what shall we do?" That is exactly what the people said to Peter (Acts 2:37).

Peter's response is so important for the Church to follow in sequence so that the Gospel path is a straight one. There are three things the Church should tell the unbeliever to do when they are ready to receive Christ:

"Repent"- This means to turn from sin and place your faith in Jesus Christ as the only answer for sin. This is the only thing needed to be saved (Mark 1:15, Luke 13:5, II Peter 3:9, Acts 20:21).

"Be baptized in the name of Jesus Christ"- This is speaking of water baptism which every new believer in Christ should do upon repentance. Back then, water baptism was actually like the sinner's prayer of today. It is a public confession of faith. Every believer in Christ today should be baptized after coming to faith in Christ. It is a commandment of the Lord (Matthew 28:19). While it is not necessary for salvation, it should come after one is saved.

"Receive the gift of the Holy Spirit"- This is speaking of the Baptism of the Holy Spirit (Luke 11:13).

Peter's main emphasis is on being saved. This should be the highest aim of all preaching, not only on the Day of Pentecost, but throughout the Church age. There were 3,000 souls who were saved on the Day of Pentecost. Interesting enough, 3,000 died on the day the Law was given (Exodus 32:28). The law kills, but grace saves!

The focus of the early Church was the apostles' doctrine, the Word of God. They were faithful to fellowship with one another and were faithful in the breaking of bread (communion). They also remained faithful to prayer (Acts 2:42-47).

This was the focus of the early Church, and it should remain the focus of the modern Church. Unfortunately, that is not the case, at least not in many churches.

The fear of God was present in the early Church due to the moving and operation of the Holy Spirit, as the Spirit was performing signs and wonders through the apostles.

The Early Church is the Model

The early Church was in unity and common belief. The early Church was a giving Church to those who had needs. We are going to have to become this kind of Church again in the coming days of great economic challenge. The early Church had a great compassion for the poor. The early Church went to the temple every day for services and they broke bread together. There was a great bond of love between the believers in the early Church. They stuck together!

The Holy Spirit had been poured out and there was great joy among the people, and the world even took notice and gave them favor. The Lord added to the Church daily souls that were being saved. It was a great revival!

There were three prayer meetings a day that took place in the early Church at the Temple in Jerusalem: 9:00 am, 12:00 pm, and 3:00 pm. The ninth hour would be the 3:00 pm prayer meeting, which was the time that Jesus died on the Cross.

In most churches today, we meet for one hour a week and *maybe* have a midweek service. We must realize that today's church doesn't look like the early Church; no wonder the modern Church is not seeing the power of God released like it did in the Book of Acts.

There is a pattern in the Book of Acts that the Bible student should take notice of. In one way or another, every move of God will take this course. Here is the progression:

1) Prayer and seeking God for a revival (Acts 1).

2) Outpouring of the Holy Spirit occurs (the Baptism with the Holy Spirit with signs following, i.e. tongues) (Acts 2).

3) Great numbers of souls are won to Jesus, 8,000 recorded (Acts 2-5).

4) Divine healing followed the move of the Holy Spirit (Acts 3).

5) Persecution from the religious world began (Acts 4).

The modern Church would do well if it read the Book of Acts and followed it. A few years ago, there was a woman who stood up and prophesied in a church in Baton Rouge, Louisiana, saying, "Read the Book of Acts and get ready!" It's one thing if a man or woman says it, but it's all together another thing if God says it!

Chapter 6

THE BAPTISM
WITH THE HOLY SPIRIT

The greatest gift that was ever given to the world was salvation. Jesus said, *"For God so loved the world, that he gave his only begotten Son, that whosoever believeth in him should not perish, but have everlasting life"* (John 3:16). But the greatest gift ever given to the Church is the Baptism with the Holy Spirit. The Bible says, *"John answered, saying unto them all, I indeed baptize you with water; but one mightier than I cometh, the latchet of whose shoes I am not worthy to unloose: he shall baptize you with the Holy Ghost and with fire"* (Luke 3:16). So John 3:16 is for the world and Luke 3:16 is for the believer after coming to Christ.

Just as vehemently as the devil works to keep the lost world from salvation, he tries to keep those who believe in Christ from the Baptism with the Holy Spirit. Why? Because he knows when one gets filled with the Holy Spirit he is going to be a bold witness for Jesus Christ (Acts 4:31).

When one gets saved, the devil knows his kingdom has shrunk by one and this is disturbing to him as he seeks to kill, steal and destroy everyone (John 10:10). He plays no favorites; he hates the whole world. But when one gets filled with the Holy Spirit, now Satan knows he is at risk of losing a whole lot more and so the Baptism with the Holy Spirit is a great threat to his kingdom.

I suppose if a believer is planning to leave this earth in a day or so, he doesn't need the Baptism with the Holy Spirit because he is going to a heavenly home soon. But, if he is planning to stay around this old sinful world for any length of time, he most definitely needs the Baptism with the Holy Spirit.

The thief on the cross didn't need to be filled with the Spirit because he was within minutes or hours of dying. What he needed was salvation. His simple confession of faith was given as he looked at Jesus who was hanging next to him on His Cross. Jesus died for the whole world, including this thief who had lived a miserable life of sin. The thief simply said, *"Lord, remember me when thou cometh into thy kingdom"* (Luke 23:42).

Those precious words spoke of remorse for the life of sin he had led and also spoke of faith that Jesus was a King and He had a kingdom. Something wonderful happened to the thief during the six hours he hung on the cross next to Jesus. The Bible says when he and the other criminal were first cruci-fied, both mocked Him (Matthew 27:38, 41-44), but something turned his sinful heart. The thief's heart was changed, and it was certainly due to viewing the suffering Christ, *"who for the joy that was set before him endured the cross, despising the shame"* (Hebrews 12:2).

The thief hung there on his cross, dying for his crimes, but witnessed the Messiah dying for the crimes (sins) of the world. When the thief exercised faith in Jesus as a King who had a kingdom, at that moment in His pain and suffering, Jesus spoke these words through His blood and tears, *"Ver-ily I say unto thee, Today shalt thou be with me in paradise"* (Luke 23:43).

The thief was saved and he didn't have time nor need to come off his cross and be water baptized or receive the Bap-tism with the Holy Ghost. He was going home; he was going to be with Jesus, along with all the departed saints that were waiting in paradise or, as it was called, "Abraham's bosom" (Luke 16:22).

Let me say it again, if you are going to live for any amount of time in this old, sinful, fallen world after you get saved, you are going to need the Baptism with the Holy Spirit which is what gives you the power to live for Christ and to minister as He directs.

What is the Baptism with the Holy Ghost?

There is much misunderstanding regarding just what the Baptism with the Holy Spirit is. If the devil can lie and misrepresent this great truth, then he has prevented many believers from experiencing greater power in their walk with Christ.

Let me first explain to you what it is not. The Baptism of the Holy Spirit is not the salvation experience. The salvation experience happens when the Holy Spirit indwells the believer or, in other words, comes into the believer's heart (Galatians 4:4-7). The Baptism with the Holy Spirit is when the Holy Spirit flows out of you in miraculous ways (Acts 1:8).

Many teach that the Baptism with the Holy Spirit happened at the moment of salvation and they will use I Corinthians 12:13 as their proof verse which reads, *"For by one Spirit are we all baptized into one body, whether we be Jews or Gentiles, whether we be bond or free;"*

The above is speaking of the salvation experience. Notice it is the Spirit (speaking of the Holy Spirit) that baptizes the believing sinner (weather Jew or Gentile), into the body of Christ at salvation.

The Baptism of the Holy Spirit is when Jesus baptizes the believer into the Holy Spirit. These are two totally different events. Notice carefully what the scriptures say as it relates to the Baptism with the Holy Spirit. John said: *"I indeed baptize you with water unto repentance: but he that cometh after me is mightier than I, whose shoes I am not worthy to bear: he shall baptize you with the Holy Ghost, and with fire"* (Matthew 3:11).

Notice the Baptizer is Jesus, the believer is the recipient, and the gift is the fullness of the Holy Spirit. In I Corinthians 12:13, the Baptizer is the Spirit and the believer is being placed into the body of Christ. Clearly these two are different. One is speaking of salvation (Romans 6:2-3), being baptized into Christ, and the other is speaking of the believer being baptized (dipped or immersed) into the Holy Spirit.

If this was the only evidence that the Baptism with the Holy Spirit was separate from the salvation experience, there might be a fair argument from those who say these events are the same. But we have much more in scripture to prove that these events - salvation (baptized into Christ's body) and the Baptism with the Holy Spirit are two entirely different experiences.

The Day of Pentecost

The Day of Pentecost was the day that the Church age began,. There were 120 who had been praying and seeking God in the upper room in Jerusalem and now were in the Temple worshipping God when *"suddenly there came a sound from heaven as of a rushing mighty wind, and it filled all the house where they were sitting"* (Acts 2:2).

This is the moment that the prophecy of John the Baptist was fulfilled (Matthew 4:11, Luke 3:16) and the prophecy of Jesus, who told them to go and wait in Jerusalem for the Promise of the Father, for He said, *"For John truly baptized with water; but ye shall be baptized with the Holy Ghost not many days hence"* (Acts 1:5).

It would actually be 10 days after Jesus gave this prophecy that they received the Baptism with the Holy Spirit, and 50 days from the crucifixion of Christ.

Some would argue that these disciples of Jesus Christ had not yet received the Holy Spirit as it pertained to salvation, so the act of being filled with the Spirit on the Day of Pentecost was their salvation experience. I don't believe the scripture bears this out. I believe they were already saved and had received the Holy Spirit for salvation.

Jesus appeared to His disciples after the resurrection on a Sunday night (the same day He was resurrected) and He said to His disciples, *"Peace be unto you: as my Father has sent me, even so send I you. And when he had said this, he breathed on them, and saith unto them, Receive ye the Holy Ghost"* (John 20:20-22).

I personally believe this was the act of the Spirit coming into the disciples' hearts, being indwelt with the Spirit (I Corinthians 12:13). The disciples were then baptized with the Holy Spirit on the Day of Pentecost when the scriptures said, *"And they were all filled with the Holy Ghost"* (Acts 2:4). Again, salvation is the Spirit coming in, but when one is filled with the Spirit, the Holy Spirit is coming in a demonstration of power.

A Demonstration of Power

We have an example of this demonstration of power in Acts chapter eight. A man by the name of Philip, who is referred to by many preachers as "Philip the Evangelist," went down to the city of Samaria and preached Christ to the unbelievers there. The people were attentive to Philip and his message regarding Jesus Christ as the Savior of the world. But Philip, filled with the Spirit, did not just preach the Gospel, there were demonstrations of the power of the Holy Spirit as miracles were happening (Acts 8:5-6).

Now this is the kind of evangelism that the early Church, filled with the Holy Spirit, demonstrated for all as a model to follow. The Apostle Paul wrote in I Corinthians 2:4-5: *"And my speech and my preaching was not with enticing words of man's wisdom, but in demonstration of the Spirit and of power: That your faith should not stand in the wisdom of men, but in the power of God."*

The Church today might have some good preachers that can impress you with their oratory ability, but in the early Church it was not the preacher that was so impressive (or his words), but it was the Holy Spirit's power that amazed the people. When the true Message of the Cross is preached through a surrendered vessel, filled with the Holy Spirit, there will be a demonstration of the Holy Spirit that follows.

This means when people hear the Gospel message spoken under the power and anointing of the Holy Spirit, there will be evidence that follows, such as salvation, deliverance, divine healing, the Baptism with the Holy Spirit, etc. This demonstration of the Spirit is what is missing in most of the modern Church.

When the Spirit is moving, the altar call which follows the preaching of the Word will sometimes be as long, or longer, than the preacher's message. This is a good sign that the preacher is operating in the Holy Spirit. But in today's church world there are precious few preachers who still give altar calls. Why? Because they are not expecting a demonstration of the Spirit or they don't know how to operate in the Spirit because they have never experienced the Baptism with the Holy Spirit. What a sad commentary indeed!

But Philip was an old-school preacher carved out of the pages of the Book of Acts and the Bible says that, after he preached, "unclean spirits" came out and people were delivered from demonic possession. Many who were sick in body, even the lame, were miraculously healed (Acts 8:7).

The Bible says there was great joy in the City of Samaria, as you can imagine there would be. Many received Philip's message of Jesus Christ and Him crucified and were saved. They were being water baptized, both men and women (Acts 8:12), which is what Jesus commanded to be done after one is saved

(Matthew 28:19). So, these were all truly converted, meaning they had been saved and baptized into the Body of Christ (John 3:3, Romans 6:3-4, I Corinthians 12:13).

At this point, the Bible shows the very next thing that needs to happen after people receive Christ as their Savior. The Scripture says, *"Now when the apostles which were at Jerusalem heard that Samaria had received the word of God, they sent unto them Peter and John: Who, when they were come down, prayed for them, that they might receive the Holy Ghost. (For as yet he was fallen upon none of them: only they were baptized in the name of the Lord Jesus.) Then laid they their hands on them, and they received the Holy Ghost"* (Acts 8:14-17).

The above scripture gives us clear evidence that salvation and receiving the Baptism with the Holy Spirit are two separate events.

As stated in the previous chapter, on the Day of Pentecost Peter got up and preached and at the end of his message he gave the three steps of what every sinner should do, who wants to be a follower of Jesus Christ (Acts 2:38-39). He said:

Step 1: "Repent"

Step 2: "Be baptized in the name of Jesus Christ" (This is speaking of water baptism)

Step 3: "You shall receive the gift of the Holy Spirit" (This is speaking of the Baptism of the Holy Spirit)

So, in this context, you can clearly see that salvation, water baptism and the Baptism with the Holy Spirit are all separate and distinct experiences within the believer's life.

There may be some who are reading this chapter and are still not convinced. Well, let me give you more examples from scripture.

The Apostle Paul

In Acts chapter 19, Paul goes to Ephesus and the Bible says he found some disciples and he asked them a very interesting question: *"have ye received the Holy Ghost since ye believed?"* (Acts 19:2) In the Greek text, this is literally, "having believed, did you receive?"

Let me ask, if it is automatic that one receives the Baptism with the Holy Spirit at conversion, then why would the apostle Paul even ask this question? It wouldn't make sense. He asked that question because he knew that they were two totally separate events, as was with his own personal experience.

Paul was converted on the road to Damascus (Acts 9:4-6) and three days later he was healed (of blindness) and filled with the Holy Spirit. The Bible says, *"And Ananias* (the man God sent to pray for Paul to receive the Baptism with the Holy Spirit) *went his way, and entered into the house* (where Paul was); *and putting his hands on him said, Brother Saul* (notice he called him "Brother" meaning he was already saved), *the Lord, even Jesus, that appeared unto thee in the way as thou camest, hath sent me, that thou mightest receive thy sight* (he was blinded by the bright light at his personal revelation of Jesus Christ, found in Acts 9:3,8), *and be filled with the Holy Ghost"* (Acts 9:17).

This is why Paul asked the disciples at Ephesus if they had received the Holy Spirit since they believed. I wonder how many today, reading this book, are saved, have been water baptized, but have not yet been filled with the Holy Spirit?

This is one of the main reasons I believe the Lord has inspired me to write this book. It is for you to clearly understand that salvation and the Baptism with the Holy Spirit are two separate events. This is one of the most revolutionary truths you will ever learn. Next to the revelation of the Cross, I don't believe there is anything more important for the believer to understand than the Baptism with the Holy Spirit.

Satan hates this truth with a passion and many religious leaders are offended at the preaching and the teaching of it. Remember, the flesh is opposed to the Spirit; they are contrary to one another (Galatians 5:17). It is God who wants this truth to be revealed to you. What I am presenting to you (through scripture) is the difference between dry, formal and stoic Christianity, and a burning fire that will make you shout, make you dance, make you weep and make you glad. It will put boldness in you and anoint you to win a lost world to Jesus (Acts 1:8).

I sense the Holy Spirit wanting me to tell you, it makes no difference who you are, preacher or lay person, Baptist, Methodist, Wesleyan, etc. Whatever your denomination or church affiliation, the Baptism with the Holy Spirit is for you. It is for every believer in Christ, for God is not one to show partiality, and what He has done for one, He will do for all. His only requirement is for you to be hungry and thirsty for more of Him (Matthew 5:6) and to believe (Acts 10:15-17).

The response of the disciples in Ephesus to Paul's question, *"Have ye received the Holy Ghost since ye believed?"* was *"We have not so much as heard whether there be any Holy Ghost"* (Acts 19:2).

Sadly enough, after almost 2,000 years since the Holy Spirit was poured out, many still have not yet heard about the gift of the Holy Spirit. Why? Simply because Satan does not want you to know or to believe in this great truth.

Paul asked another question to get more information from these disciples, *"Unto what then were ye baptized? And they said, Unto John's baptism"* (Acts 19:3). Notice that Paul used the term "baptism" after they said they didn't hear about any Holy Spirit. So, clearly Paul's question *"have ye received the Holy Ghost since you believed?"* is referring to the Baptism with the Holy Spirit.

Now when Paul knew they had not yet been baptized with the Holy Spirit, he questioned what they knew and upon finding out that they were disciples of John and had not even been water baptized in Jesus' name, he explained to them the difference between John's message and Jesus' message. Upon hearing Paul, the Bible says they were water baptized in the name of the Lord Jesus, thus confessing publicly they were now followers of Jesus Christ.

After being water baptized the Bible says, *"And when Paul had laid his hands upon them, the Holy Ghost came on them; and they spake with tongues, and prophesied"* (Acts 19:6).

The scriptural evidence that we have presented should convince you that the salvation experience and the experience of being baptized with the Holy Spirit are two separate and distinct events in the Christian life. But as C.S. Lewis once said, "There is enough evidence for a non-believer to come to Christ, but there is not enough evidence for the non-believer who will not come." I will say then that there is enough evidence for the Baptism of the Holy Spirit to be received, but not enough evidence for the one who doesn't want to receive.

One Baptism, Many Fillings

When one speaks of being baptized with the Holy Spirit, we are speaking of the initial infilling of the Holy Spirit or what it means to be "filled with the Holy Spirit." Notice when Jesus prophesied about the Baptism with the Holy Spirit (Acts 1:5), and that prophecy was actually fulfilled (10 days later), the scriptures define it as *"they were all filled with the Holy Ghost"* (Acts 2:4).

The Bible says in Ephesians 5:18, *"And be not drunk with wine, wherein is excess; but be filled with the Spirit."* This actually means in the Greek text "but be constantly controlled by the Spirit" or in other words "be continually filled." There is one initial Baptism with the Holy Spirit, but many refillings.

In Acts 4, the disciples who had already been baptized with the Holy Spirit, were praying to God for boldness and were refilled with the Spirit. The scripture says, *"and they were all filled with the Holy Ghost, and they spake the word of God with boldness"* (Acts 4:31).

Many years ago, when my wife and I were first married, we were given a gift by some close friends to go to a very beautiful winter getaway in Canada. I will never forget the first time we went. It was so beautiful and peaceful. We were able to relax and be refreshed from the heavy schedule we were keeping with our ministry.

This vacation made such an impression on us that we would return every year around the same time to spend a few days of time alone together. We have gone back many times, but there was still only one first time. Such it is with being filled with the Holy Spirit: one first time (Spirit Baptism), and many fillings after that. As one man said, we have one major problem as Christians - we leak and need to be refilled constantly.

The Initial Evidence That One Has Been Filled

I believe the scriptures teach that every time one is baptized with the Holy Spirit, he or she will receive the ability to speak in other tongues (languages that previously were unknown by that person). This is a supernatural gift and one that the Lord uses to give the recipient confirmation that he or she has been filled.

This supernatural sign "speaking with other tongues" was prophesied by Isaiah some 800 years before Christ. He said *"For with stammering lips and another tongue will he speak to this people"* (Isaiah 28:11). This phrase "stammering lips," refers to a proper language being spoken, but yet the people hearing it would not understand it.[1]

Paul referred to this prophecy in I Corinthians 14:21-22 and said the gift of tongues was a sign to unbelievers. This was exactly how it was used on the Day of Pentecost when the newly Spirit-filled disciples came out of the Temple speaking in other languages. The unbelievers who were there heard them speak in their own native languages. Yet they were perplexed, knowing that the people who were speaking were Galileans, (they had Galilean accents) and some were amazed, some were in doubt and some mocked (Acts 2:5-13).

This strange occurrence in Jerusalem had never been seen or heard before. But Paul, speaking of the prophecy of Isaiah, said it had been predicted long ago by the prophet.

This commotion of people speaking in languages they had never learned before was the sign gift that God used to show the world that the Holy Spirit was being poured out, just as it had been prophesied would happen in the last days (Joel 2:28-29).

Why Tongues?

Someone once asked why God chose speaking in tongues as the initial evidence that one had been filled. I don't know if I have a complete answer to give you, but I do believe we have some evidence as to why the Godhead chose to use the speaking in other languages as the evidence, or the sign gift, that one has been filled with the Spirit.

We have to go back to Genesis chapter 11 and look at the Tower of Babel where the scripture tells us that *"the whole earth was of one language, and of one speech"* (Genesis 11:1). We do not know what that one language was because the scripture doesn't tell us, but many believe it was Hebrew due to the fact that this was the language of God's chosen people.

There was a prince at this time named Nimrod (kind of a funny name, but not funny in that day), who was a very evil man and ruled in Babylon. In this city many people came together in unity (not God's unity), and decided to build a tower. This tower would be built as high as possible (man was planning to reach heaven).

Their motive for building this was one of pride as they said, *"let us make us a name, lest we be scattered abroad upon the face of the whole earth"* (Genesis 11:4). In this one verse we see the rebellion against God. In fact, this was the very first organized rebellion against God. The Lord wanted mankind to be scattered over the Earth (Genesis 9:1), but these rebels were determined to defy what God desired.[2]

The Bible says that the Lord came down from the third heaven to see the city and the tower that these men had built against His Word. The Lord said, *"Behold, the people is one, and they have all one language; and this they begin to do: and now nothing will be restrained from them, which they have imagined to do"* (Genesis 11:6).

Because the people built this city and this tower without the consultation or direction of God, the Lord was grieved by their independence and their unity apart from Him. He knew their rebellion and their evil had no limits.

In order to disrupt their evil plans, God confused the languages. God said, *"Go to, let us* (speaking of the Trinity) *go down, and there confound their language, that they may not understand one another's speech"* (Genesis 11:7). As a result of the scattering of the languages, the name of the city and the tower were called "Babel" which means "confusion," which is also the Hebrew name for "Babylon."[3]

So the city of "Babel," with its tower of "Babel," is forever known as the place where man tried to unite without God and God, in turn, brought confusion to them by scattering the languages.

But on the Day of Pentecost, God supernaturally gave the gift of language (i.e. speaking with other tongues) as the sign gift. The Lord reunited men in the "unity of the Spirit." That is why the Bible, when speaking of unity, only speaks of one unity that God will accept and that is the *"unity of the Spirit"* (Eph. 4:3-6).

It is only the Holy Spirit Baptism, with the evidence of speaking with other tongues, that brings the true unity of the

Spirit. In Genesis 11, we see the unity of man (attempted without God) at the tower of Babel came to an end as God divided man by the speaking of other tongues or languages. In Acts 2, however, the unity of God, which unifies man by the Spirit, is evidenced by the speaking with other tongues or languages.

Isn't it interesting that some who have opposed tongues today call the gift a "bunch of babel"? For that is what God called the city and tower that man built without Him. But God calls the speaking with other tongues the evidence of the outpouring of the Holy Spirit, which was prophesied by Joel so long ago (Acts 2:16-21).

The Greatest Blessing of Being Baptized with the Holy Spirit

The greatest blessing of being baptized with the Holy Spirit is not the ability to speak in other tongues, as wonderful and as powerful as that gift is. Tongues is simply the evidence. The greatest blessing of the Baptism with the Holy Spirit is that one is drawn closer to Jesus Christ.

Everything in the Christian life becomes bigger and more meaningful after you have been baptized with the Holy Spirit. Your love for God gets bigger, your love for souls gets bigger, your conviction of sin grows deeper, your love for scripture grows wider, etc., etc.

I loved the Bible after I was saved, but when I was baptized with the Holy Spirit I couldn't put it down. I loved souls after I was saved, but I wept for them more after I was baptized with the Holy Spirit. I had conviction in my heart regarding personal purity after I was saved, but when I was baptized with the Holy Spirit my desire for personal holiness deepened.

After I was baptized with the Holy Spirit I also began to experience the moving and operation of the Holy Spirit in a more dynamic way than I ever had before. The gifts of the

Spirit started operating in my life, and I began to see miracles take place in my life that were simply amazing.

The Baptism with the Holy Spirit is exactly as advertised. The Greek word for "Baptism" is "baptizo" and it means "to dip, to immerse, submerge for a religious purpose, to overwhelm, saturate." The word means to completely and totally immerse an object into a substance to the point that when it is brought out of that substance it has been changed and now resembles that substance into which it was submerged.

So, the Baptism with the Holy Spirit is speaking of being immersed into the Holy Spirit, and once you experience it you are going to resemble more of who Jesus Christ is. The recipient of the Baptism with the Holy Spirit will testify of a deeper love for Jesus, deeper love for souls, deeper desire to study the scriptures, supernatural signs that take place in their life, etc.

The waters of Baptism with the Holy Spirit will "overwhelm" you and take you from the "ankle deep" into the depths where you will be changed forever. Evan Roberts was a man God used greatly in the Welsh revival at the turn of the 20th century. He said these words toward the end of his life, "The essence of revival is the Baptism with the Holy Spirit."

Every child of God needs to be baptized with the Holy Spirit with the evidence of speaking with other tongues. It is biblical and it is the Promise of God for all generations. Acts 2:39 says, *"For the promise is unto you, and to your children, and to all that are afar off, even as many as the Lord our God shall call."*

Chapter 7

THE GIFTS OF THE HOLY SPIRIT

Paul wrote to the Corinthian Church and said these words: *"Follow after charity and desire spiritual gifts"* (I Cor.14:1). How many in the modern Church desire to receive spiritual gifts? *How many even know that God desires to give them spiritual gifts?* The answer would be not many. However, God encourages His Church to desire to see supernatural gifts operating in His Church.

Why would Christians not desire spiritual gifts? Many today have limited God and don't believe the same spiritual gifts that the early Church operated in are still in operation today. However, there is no scriptural evidence to justify such a position. Due to ignorance and unbelief, many have missed God and the Church has been weakened and proven powerless. This is a sad reality of today's Church, but for all those reading this book, please understand that God has not changed. In Malachi 3:6, God said, *"For I am the Lord, I change not,"* He still wants His children to operate in the spiritual gifts as did the early Church.

Gifts From the Holy Spirit

There is a woman in the Bible named Rebekah who was chosen by God to be the wife of Isaac. How she was chosen is one of the most amazing stories in the Bible. In Genesis 24, Abraham is mourning the death of his wife, Sarah. He brings in his oldest, most trusted servant, Eliezer, and gives him instructions to go and find the mate in Nahor (700 miles away) that God has for his son, Isaac.

Eliezer puts out a "fleece" (a way to know God's will) to the Lord that the first woman to come to the well and give him and his ten camels a drink would be the one whom God had chosen for Isaac. This was a pretty strong fleece, knowing how much camels can drink, but Eliezer had to be sure he brought back the woman that God had chosen for his master's son. The seriousness of this journey was such that the very lineage of the Messiah was at stake.

Rebekah did, in fact, come to the well, and did, in fact, offer to give Eliezer and his camels a drink. She actually was the great niece of Abraham and was God's choice to become Isaac's wife. God answered Eliezer's request just as he had asked.

Understanding Bible typology, this story takes on a much bigger meaning, as this is a type of our salvation. It is a beautiful picture of God reaching man. Abraham is a type of God the Father, as he is called the "Father of many nations." Sarah, his wife who was "laid aside" in death, is a type of Israel. Isaac, Abraham's son, is a type of the Lord Jesus Christ. (If you remember Abraham was asked to sacrifice his one and only son in Genesis 22.) Rebekah is a type of the Church and the servant Eliezer, whose name means "My God is a Helper," is a type of the Holy Spirit. The Holy Spirit is the "Comforter" which actually means "the Helper" (John 14:26).

Just as Eliezer had to go a mighty long way to find Rebekah (again, a type of the Church), God came a long way to reach us. The Bible says that Eliezer had to wait at the well for Rebekah (Gen. 24:13). He is a type of the Holy Spirit, who is patient and waits until we repent of our sins and come to the well (living water of God).

The ten camels of Abraham that traveled with Eliezer (Genesis 24:10) were carrying some of the riches of Abraham that Eliezer would present as gifts to the one who was to be Isaac's wife. In Genesis 24:22, the Bible says that Eliezer gave Rebekah a golden earring and two golden bracelets. This is a type of the spiritual gifts that God gives His bride when we accept Him. God is a good God and He wants to give His people spiritual gifts.

There are nine spiritual gifts spoken of in I Corinthians 12, and nine is the number of the Holy Spirit. Realize there are more than nine gifts that God Almighty gives to His Church (Romans 12:6-8), but the Holy Spirit singled out nine spiritual gifts in I Corinthians 12. They are the Word of Wisdom, Word of Knowledge, Gift of Faith, Gifts of Healing, the Working of Miracles, Prophecy, Discerning of Spirits, Divers Kinds of Tongues and Interpretation of Tongues.

These spiritual gifts are sometimes referred to as "tools of power." They are called that because they accompany the Baptism with the Holy Spirit, which is the power of the Holy Spirit to assist the believer in being a bold witness to a lost world.

The word "gifts" in the Greek is "charismata" and means "grace." It is where we get the word "charismatic." Every gift given by God is because of grace. We have not earned anything, but because of the Cross and our faith in what Jesus did there, we have received the gift of the Holy Spirit into our lives and He, like Eliezer, brings the gifts of the Spirit with Him.

The Bible says in I Corinthains 12:7: *"But the manifestation of the Spirit is given to every man to profit withal."* The word in the Greek for "manifestation" is "phaneros" and it simply means "open to view, visible, or make known." The manifestation of the Spirit is meant to help Christians meet needs. A Christian, walking in the Spirit, ministers to another individual by utilizing specific gifts.[1]

The reason the gifts are distributed to believers is for the common good of man (I Cor. 12:7) and for the glorification of Jesus Christ (I Cor. 12:3). They are not for man's use or his glory. They are *God's* gifts for His purpose and glory. Now there are diversities of gifts, meaning different types, but it is the same Holy Spirit that distributes them. One Giver, many gifts.

There are also differences of operations (I Cor. 12:6), which means there are different ways the Holy Spirit works. All of the gifts of the Spirit are important. <u>Without the gifts of the Spirit the Church cannot operate in supernatural power the way it was intended to, and becomes nothing more than a human organization.</u>

A church may have a beautiful building, many different programs, a large choir and a large ministry team with many full-time pastors, but if it does not have the power of the Holy Spirit moving in it, that church will have little impact on the people in it and the world.

When a man is bound by demonic powers, he doesn't need a beautiful church or nice program, but he needs a man or woman of God who is filled with the power of the Holy Spirit to lay their hands on him, bind that demon spirit and send it out of him in the name of Jesus Christ of Nazareth. The Bible says it is the "anointing that breaks the yoke" (Isaiah 10:27).

A good friend of mine named Bob has one of the most amazing testimonies I think I have ever heard. When Bob was a teenager he was heavily involved with drugs and became a drug pusher as well as a user. He had a pretty big enterprise going on the streets of South Buffalo back in the 1970's. His drug habit became so bad that he stopped eating and his body began to fail him. The demons that were allowed to torment him would sometimes thrash him around in his bed while he was asleep. It got so bad that he was afraid to go to sleep so he just walked the streets all night.

He came to the point where he had severe chest pains and would feel like he was about to have a major heart attack. His eyes had dark circles underneath them and his head hurt so bad that he could not even touch the tips of his hair without pain. His teeth were rotting out of his mouth. He looked so bad that he was afraid to look in the mirror and the last time he looked in a mirror he saw the face of a demon. It scared him so badly that he refused to look at himself again.

Bob's drug habit had taken its toll and he was at the end of his rope. His very life was now at stake. One day he heard a voice say, "Bobby, if you don't do something today, you will not see tomorrow."

He knew the voice was correct, he could feel his body slipping away and his soul close to departing. He was afraid and desperate. The demons of hell had come to pull him into the place of torment forever. Bob had reached his wretched man moment (Romans 7:24). He thought to himself, what can I do?

It was then that he remembered a small group of teenagers who would meet in a store front for Bible study. He had tried many times to sell them drugs but to no avail. He immediately began to run through the streets of South Buffalo to this little store front Bible study. He said it was only the grace of God that allowed him to run so fast without dying before he got there.

When he arrived at the front door, he looked in the window and to his amazement they were all there. He busted through the door and all the teens snapped their heads around only to see Bobby. He said they had a look of fear on their faces. They had no idea what he wanted. They only knew him as the neighborhood's biggest drug dealer.

Bobby looked at the Bible study leader, a petite woman, and said these words, "If your God is real then I need Him right now." The Spirit-filled lady who led the Bible study came boldly over to him and she laid her hands on the top of his head and said, "in the name of Jesus." Bob said he never heard another word. The next thing he knew he was laying on the ground and all the kids were looking at him as if they were seeing a ghost.

The little lady was dancing and jumping, praising God like a fanatic. He didn't know what happened. But they said to Bobby "go look in a mirror, go look in a mirror." They didn't know that was Bobby's greatest fear. They finally convinced him to go look in the mirror. When he looked he couldn't believe his eyes. The dark circles under his eyes were gone. In fact, his eyes were clear and bright and his face was shining. He smiled to look at his teeth and they had all been restored. Bob was instantly set free from drugs; his body was healed. There was no pain in his chest or head. It was a miracle. He stayed up all night in that little store. He got saved and that same night received the Baptism with the Holy Spirit with the evidence of speaking with other tongues. It was just like the book of Acts. God literally saved and delivered Bob's life.

Today, he is one of most loving and anointed youth pastors I have ever met. He and his wife have served faithfully in a South Buffalo church where the woman who God used to set him free still pastors with her husband. Only God knows how many young people have been reached for Christ through Bobby's ministry.

Bob, at his lowest point, ready to die, didn't need a program or a beautiful building. What he needed was a God-called, God-gifted servant who knew the power of the Holy Spirit. This is what our churches need, this is what our youth ministries need, this is what America needs, this is what Canada needs, and this is what the world needs.

Understanding the Gifts of the Spirit

Many Christians do not understand the gifts of the Spirit. Paul said to the Corinthian Church, *"Now concerning spiritual gifts, brethren, I would not have you ignorant"* (I Cor. 12:1). Many churches today are dying spiritually because they don't understand the gifts of the Spirit and therefore don't desire them and don't operate in them.

The Lord spoke through the Prophet Hosea and said: *"My people are destroyed for lack of knowledge"* (Hosea 4:6). The word knowledge here means "understanding gained by actual experience." Most of the people in the modern Church of America and Canada have never experienced the Baptism with the Holy Spirit as the disciples did on the Day of Pentecost (and throughout the Book of Acts). This is due to them lacking the knowledge of it. The truth is, their church doesn't preach it because either their pastor doesn't believe it is for today or he ignores it all together.

Hosea said the reason why God's people of his day lacked the knowledge was *"because thou hast rejected knowledge."* Anytime a believer denies the Baptism with the Holy Spirit, which means he is denying the power of God, he will never be able to understand the gifts of the Spirit. The Baptism with the Holy Spirit is the "gateway" to spiritual gifts.

Paul didn't give us much wiggle room when it comes to dealing with people in the Church who deny the power of God. He gave some clear and concise instructions to Timothy (Pastor of the Church at Ephesus), when he said, *"Having a form of godliness, but denying the power thereof: from such turn away"* (II Tim. 3:5).

The purpose of the spiritual gifts is to exalt the name of Jesus Christ and to draw people closer to Him. The gifts are never meant to puff up the person whom God is using in the exercise of spiritual gifts, but unfortunately this has been the case in far too many churches. God's Word says, *"And though I have the gift of prophecy, and understand all mysteries, and all knowledge; and though I have all faith, so that I could remove mountains, and have not charity* (love)*, I am nothing"* (I Cor.13:2).

Loving God and loving others is the most important characteristic of the Christian life. If the love of God and of others is motivating the one who is operating in spiritual gifts, that one will not be puffed up. The Word of God, in describing what love is, says that love *"is not puffed up"* (I Cor. 13:4). One should always remember that spiritual gifts are always meant to help others (I Cor. 12:7) and bring glory to God.

God distributes His gifts on whom He wills, when He wills. The Bible says, *"But all these worketh that one and the selfsame Spirit, dividing to every man severally as he will"* (I Cor.12:11).

All the spiritual gifts are to proclaim to a lost and dying world that Jesus is Lord. Paul said, *"Wherefore I give you to understand, that no man speaking by the Spirit of God calleth Jesus accursed: and that no man can say that Jesus is the Lord, but by the Holy Ghost"* (I Cor. 12:3). All the gifts are aimed at exalting Jesus Christ as the Lord.

Many people in churches today have abused the gifts of the Spirit because they have left Christ and the Cross as the object of their Christian faith. Anytime you leave the Cross, you will lose your perspective and misunderstand and misuse the things of God.

Paul warned the Corinthian Church about its past of worshipping "dumb idols" and the implication is they are not to do that with the spiritual gifts (I Cor. 12:2). However, much of the Pentecostal and Charismatic Church have done just that. This, again, is due to taking the its focus off of Jesus Christ and Him crucified (I Cor. 2:2).

Whenever the Church moves away from the Cross, it is, in essence, separating Jesus from the Cross. When you separate Jesus from the Cross you are creating "another Jesus" (II Cor.11:4).

Classifications of Gifts

Bible scholars and theologians have separated the nine gifts of the Spirit into three classifications. First, there are the Revelation Gifts, which are the gifts of the Spirit that "reveal something" that was previously hidden or unknown. Second, there are the Power Gifts, which are gifts of the Spirit that "do something." In the third classification are the Vocal Gifts, which are the gifts of the Spirit that "say something."

These classifications are to help you better understand what each gift is meant to accomplish. The three classifications are listed below, along with the gifts that fit in each category. We will take a look at each classification in the next few chapters.

Revelation Gifts

1) Word of Wisdom

2) Word of Knowledge

3) Discerning of Spirits

Power Gifts

1) Gift of Faith

2) Gifts of Healing

3) Working of Miracles

Vocal Gifts

1) Prophecy

2) Divers Kinds of Tongues

3) Interpretation of Tongues

Chapter 8

THE REVELATION GIFTS

Word of Wisdom

The first gift of the Spirit listed is the "Word of Wisdom." The Word of Wisdom is not called the Gift of Wisdom because it is a "word" that God gives, and not a continuous flow of wisdom. The wisdom given through this gift is a supernatural revelation regarding the plan of God, and not day-to-day wisdom.

The Word of Wisdom is the mind of God pertaining to a futuristic event. In my opinion, it is an amazing gift. Why? Because anyone who can have prior knowledge to a futuristic event is at a great advantage and can be used of God mightily.

Jesus foretold events on many occasions, telling the people what would be the sign of His second coming. He prophesied the destruction of the Temple in 70 AD, and He foretold His own death and His resurrection. This gift is powerful as it can cause the unbeliever to stand up and listen.

Some years ago, I was coaching football at a particular high school and we made it to the playoffs. In fact, we were one win away from playing for a Section Championship. The team we had to play were two-time State Champions and going for their third State title in a row. We had not beaten this team in ten years and, needless to say, we needed to play a perfect game if we expected to win.

A few hours before the game, I was driving in my car and all of sudden I had a vision. I saw all of our players and fans running on the field and jumping on each other. As I saw this happening in my mind's eye, I said out loud, "Oh Lord, we just beat Jamestown," (the name of the team we were going to play).

I called my wife to tell her what the Lord had just shown me. I don't know if she believed me, but she found my call intriguing to say the least. I wondered why the Lord gave me this prophetic vision; this Word of Wisdom. What was the purpose for it? What was the reason the Holy Spirit would want me to see the victory before it actually happened?

As our team was in the locker room preparing to come out for the introduction of the players, I thought of my vision and it gave me great confidence. One of our players asked me if I would give a little sermon before the game. They had grown accustomed to me leading them in prayer and preaching to them. The head coach gave me the freedom to speak about Jesus and pray with the team even though it was a public school. I had great favor at this particular school where I coached for ten seasons. The head coach at that school was, and is, an amazing man whom I love very much.

I went into the player's locker room before the game, and they were all sitting there in full equipment with their helmets on and the lights turned off. I had only about three minutes to give my sermon. I preached the story of Moses parting the Red Sea. I told the offensive line that they needed to open holes for Ty (our running back), the way God opened the Red Sea for the Israelites to pass through. I told the defense that they needed to close the holes the way God closed the Red Sea on the Egyptians. The team got so excited by what I shared that they started pounding on the lockers and yelling "let's go!" I settled them down and we took a knee to pray.

As I came out of the locker room and stood in the end zone waiting for the introduction of the players, I looked over and saw the head coach's wife standing there. All of a sudden I felt a boldness come over me to tell her what God had shown me. I walked over to her and I said, "Robin, tonight we are going to beat Jamestown and when we do all the fans are going to run on the field to celebrate. I want you to come out on the field and celebrate too." She gave me a strange look and then said, "Ok Mike, if we win and the fans do what you say, I will come on the field and celebrate too."

Now, you have to remember two things. First, we hadn't beaten this team in ten years and secondly, they were two-time State Champions. Also, I should point out that in all the years I had coached at this school, the fans had never rushed onto the field after a game. The security at our games was pretty tight and they never let the student body come onto the field. So, now you know why she looked at me so strangely; my prediction seemed really "out there" for her as you might imagine.

As the game came to the end, Jamestown scored with less than one minute to go, and took the lead by six points. I thought to myself, "Lord, how is my vision going to come true? Did I really hear from you? Was that vision from you or not?"

We got the ball, and the first three downs were incomplete passes. There were only seconds left in the game, it was fourth down and we were on our own 20 yard line. I thought the only thing we can do is throw up the "Hail Jesus," (that is always better than "Hail Mary"), and pray. I started to pace the side-lines and began questioning my vision. I thought, "How will I be able to face the coach's wife after being so confident about my prediction?" I was very confused.

I walked over to see what play the coach was telling our quarterback to call. I couldn't believe my ears when, on fourth down with no timeouts and on our own 20 yard line, he called a running play. In my mind I said, "He gave up. Coach gave up!" I was so discouraged.

Then, the unexpected happened. The center snapped the ball to our quarterback and he pitched it to our running back (Ty) who began to run around the end and down our sidelines, breaking tackles as he went. I ran down the sideline screaming, "Go Ty, Go!" To my amazement, he ran 80 yards for the touchdown. What an incredible call by our coach! We kicked the extra point and won the game by one point. All the fans came pouring onto the field at the conclusion of the game. We beat Jamestown for the first time in ten years, and we were going to the Sectional Championship (which we would go on to win), and the vision that I saw, just hours before the game, was totally and completely right on! Praise God!

As the players and coaches hugged each other, I looked up and there, standing at about the 50 yard line with her hands folded, staring right at me, was the coach's wife. Her look was one of shock and awe. She never said anything to me, but her look said it all. It was as if she was saying, "Who are you? How did you know?"

Many of the prophecies in the Old Testament were actually Words of Wisdom. They were given to the prophets pertaining to futuristic events.[1] We will explain the difference between the Word of Wisdom and the gift of Prophecy when we discuss the gift of Prophecy.

Word of Knowledge

The gift of the Word of Knowledge is also under the category of "Revelation Gifts," as it reveals something previously or presently unknown to the one operating in the gift.

Just as with the gift of the Word of Wisdom, the gift of the Word of Knowledge is not called the Gift of Knowledge, but it is called the "Word of Knowledge," so this is not day-to-day knowledge, but is a supernatural revelation given by God to assist in a certain situation. The Word of Knowledge differs from the Word of Wisdom in that this special revelation pertains to past or present events while the Word of Wisdom has to do with future events.

We see Jesus operating in the Word of Knowledge in John chapter 4. He met a woman at the well in Samaria and He asked her to give Him a drink, which was a shock to her because at that time it was unusual for a Jew to talk to a Samaritan, let alone a Samaritan woman. Jesus began to witness to the woman regarding eternal life. He used water as His symbol for everlasting life and He told her He had water that, if she drank of it, she would never be thirsty again (He was speaking spiritually).

The woman said, *"Sir, give me this water, that I thirst not"* (John 4:15). Jesus then said to her, *"Go call thy husband, and come hither"* (John 4:16). The woman told Jesus that she had no husband and then Jesus, operating in the Word of Knowledge, told her that she spoke correctly by saying she has no husband, but previously she had five husbands and the man that she is living with now is not her husband (John 4:17-18).

Upon hearing the Word of Knowledge operating in Jesus, the woman said unto Him, *"Sir, I perceive that thou art a prophet"* (John 4:19). It was the gift of the Spirit operating in Jesus that caused the woman to believe that Jesus was a Prophet of God. Spiritual gifts build faith in unbelievers.

Jesus went on to minister to her about who is a true worshipper of God and He proclaimed to her that salvation is of the Jews. The woman responded to Jesus by saying, *"I know that Messiah cometh, which is called Christ: when He is come, he will tell, us all things"* (John 4:25). Jesus replied, *"I that speak unto thee am he"* (John 4:26).

The Samaritan woman left her water pot and went back into her city and said to the men there, *"Come, see a man, which told me all things that ever I did: is not this the Christ?"*

(John 4:29). And the Bible says the men (probably the women and children as well) came to see Jesus and the Bible says they *"believed on him for the saying of the woman, which testified, He told me all that ever I did"* (John 4:39). The Word of Knowledge operating in Jesus brought a crowd.

Jesus stayed with the people for two days and many believed in Jesus after hearing Him teach. They testified, saying to the woman, *"Now we believe, not because of thy saying: for we have heard him ourselves, and know that this is indeed the Christ, the Savior of the world"* (John 4:42).

This is a beautiful example of the power of the Holy Spirit working through the gifts of the Spirit (i.e. the Word of Knowledge).

There are many Christians whom God has used through the centuries to operate in the Word of Knowledge and have literally shocked the unbeliever to say, "how did you know that?" To which the answer can only be, "God revealed it to me!" The Word of Knowledge is a great gift in the work of evangelism as we see so obviously in the story of the woman from Samaria.

My best friend in elementary school was a guy named Joe. We did everything together. We played sports together, got in trouble together and went everywhere together. When we graduated from grammar school, my mother was so glad that we were going to different schools because she was convinced that we were not a good influence on each other. A few days before high school was to begin, I received a call from Joe and he told me that he was going to the same private school as I was. My Mom was not too happy, even though she really liked Joe.

We both went out for the football team, I became the quarterback and Joe became the wide receiver. We had a lot of success together on the field, mainly because we practiced together all the time. I loved hanging with Joe. But later in high school, we grew apart and after high school we lost track of each other. After I got saved, God gave me a burden for him and he was number one on my most wanted list for salvation. I would pray for him often.

One night I had a dream about him and a few days later I ran into him. I really felt the Lord wanted me to share Christ with him but I didn't. I guess I was afraid he would reject Christ and reject me. I felt very discouraged by my lack of boldness.

It was about a year later that I had another dream about Joe, and, sure enough, a day or two later I ran into him again. This time I knew that the dreams were connected to me seeing him, and that God wanted me to share Christ with him. Unfortunately, I failed to share Christ with him again. This time it really troubled me. So often it is the people closest to you that are the hardest ones to share Christ with.

Thank God for the grace and patience of the Lord. Another year or so passed and I had my third dream and this one was very specific. In the dream, Joe was very depressed as he and his wife were getting a divorce, and he was thinking about taking his own life. To my amazement, the next day I saw Joe again. Wow! God is amazing!

This time I had to share my faith with him. So, I said to him, "Joe, I had a dream about you last night. In my dream you were getting a divorce from your wife and you were thinking about taking your own life. Is there any truth to this dream?"

I saw tears well up in his eyes as he said, "Your dream is exactly right on." He invited me back to his house and I shared my faith with him for over two hours. The Word of Knowledge is powerful in the work of evangelism. We serve a supernatural God who loves the whole world and wants all men to be saved (John 3:16, II Peter 3:9).

Discerning of Spirits

Another revelation gift is the "Discerning of Spirits." This is a very important gift as it is used to protect the Church from evil and fleshly abuses. The word "discernment" in the Greek is "anakrino" and it means "to distinguish, or separate out so as to investigate by looking throughout objects or particulars, hence signifies to examine, scrutinize, question, to hold a preliminary judicial examination."[2] It basically means to judge if something is good or evil.

Today, the greatest need in the Church is discernment, but it is lacking in so many denominations and churches. Why is this? I believe it comes down to believers not studying the Bible to show themselves approved unto God (II Tim. 2:15) and denying the power of the Holy Spirit, who is the One who gives us discernment.

Spiritual laziness leads Christians to look to man or a church to discern the Word of God for them. But the Bible says that we are to study for ourselves, and, in fact, we will each be accountable unto God for what we know and what we don't know. Paul said three different times in Romans 6 and 7, "Know ye not" or "Don't you know."

There are three levels of discernment. First, there is "natural discernment." This is the ordinary wisdom of a man who can spot obvious danger and react to it. You don't have to be saved to have this kind of discernment. I grew up in the city, and there were friends that I had that we would say had a lot of "street smarts." They just had the ability on the streets to know who they could trust and who they couldn't. The natural man can possess this kind of discernment. A lot of times, we see mothers who just know things about their children and we call that a "mother's intuition." This is "natural discernment" and can be found in a non-believer as well as a Christian.

The next level of discernment is called "biblical discernment." You must be born again to possess this type of discernment. This is the kind of discernment whereby a person, who has studied his Bible, can make spiritual decisions based on his knowledge of the Word of God. As a person walks with God, continues to study the Word of God and experiences more and more of the spiritual life with Christ, his or her biblical discernment will grow. The Bible says:

"For every one that useth milk is unskillful in the word of righteousness: for he is a babe. But strong meat belongeth to them that are of full age, even those who by reason of use have their senses exercised to discern both good and evil" (Heb. 5:13-14).

The third level of discernment is one of the nine gifts of the Spirit and it is called the "Discerning of Spirits." Now, this supernatural gift is another level of discernment that pertains to the spirit world. This supernatural assistance allows the Christian to detect if a person, idea, or direction is of a human spirit (of the flesh), demonic spirit (of the devil) or the Holy Spirit. This gift will enable the person to discern the motive behind an individual or a situation. Also, the Discerning of Spirits can even give the ability to actually see into the "spirit world."

Elisha prayed that God would open the eyes of his servant and he would see into the spirit realm. The Lord answered his prayer and the servant's eyes were opened and he saw the mountain was full of horses and chariots of fire round about Elisha (II Kings 6:17). The servant learned there was a whole other world unseen by men that existed all around them. It is called the "spirit world."

A friend of mine told me one time while he was searching for God, he walked into a Mormon Church (which is a false way that adds to, and takes away from, the true Word of God) and he saw, in the Spirit, a black cloud filling the room. He went back to the church later that night for a service and God opened his eyes again and he saw the head of a demon on one of the people in the church. He immediately ran out of that church and never returned.

Many times when the gift of Discerning of Spirits is in operation, the Word of Knowledge will be also, and God will reveal to the person certain truths that he does not know. I remember one summer my family was attending a summer Christian festival and I was teaching young people under a tent each day of the festival. I would go home to sleep each night, as we lived only about 45 minutes away, but my wife and kids camped out at the festival.

One morning I got up and sought the Lord in prayer for a while before I had to leave to go the festival. I went down into my basement to iron the clothes I was going to wear that day. After ironing my clothes, I went back upstairs, got dressed and left for the festival.

When I went outside to get into my car, (it was a very hot and humid day), I realized I was not wearing the right clothes. I was very uncomfortable and I had only been in the sun for a brief time, so I quickly went back in the house to change. When I went back downstairs into the basement to iron my new set of clothes, I saw something that startled me. Lying on the small strip of carpeting by the ironing board, where I had been standing just a few moments earlier, was a mask. It actually was a mask from the Bible Man costume that we had bought for our son some years before. He had not worn it for a long time as he had grown older. I am not even sure where we had stored it. Bible Man is a Christian hero on a kids TV show. His character defeated the forces of evil by quoting the Word of God.

I walked over to the mask and picked it up and held it in my hand. At first I felt fear come over me as I said these words out loud, "somebody is down here." However, there was no one at home but me. My whole family was at the Christian festival. So, I instantly had to discern whether it was an angel, a demon or a human being who had put that mask in that spot so I would clearly see it when I came down the stairs.

I believe the Lord gave me His gift of discernment as I was confident it was an angel that had placed that mask in that spot. As I held the mask in my hand I said, "There is an angel down here." When I said that, I instantly sensed the presence of the Holy Spirit come over me. I asked the Lord, "Lord, what are you trying to say to me?" I felt the Lord say that He wanted me to be like Bible Man and know the Word of God so well that I could stand against the forces of evil that came against me. The attacks from the evil world are real, and God has given us the sword of the Spirit as an offensive weapon (Eph. 6:17) against the devil and his henchmen. He has also given us the shield of faith (Eph. 6:16) whereby we are able to quench all the fiery darts of the wicked.

Jesus said, *"Verily I say unto you, Whatsoever ye shall bind on earth shall be bound in heaven and whatsoever ye shall loose on earth shall be loosed in heaven" (Matt. 18:18).*

Jesus also said, *"Behold, I give unto you power to tread on serpents and scorpions, and over all the power of the enemy: and nothing shall by any means hurt you" (Luke 10:19).*

The above verses tell us that God can give us spiritual authority over spirit beings (i.e. demon spirits). We must realize that, as Christians, we are no match for the devil, but the devil is no match for the power of the Holy Ghost.

After my Bible mask experience, I left for the Christian festival, but I have to admit to you that I first checked every part of my house to make sure there was no intruder. I wanted to completely rule out man's involvement in this bizarre happening. However, more would happen that day that would give me even further insight into the mask.

Later that same day, I was preaching in a tent filled with about 300 young people and adults. All of a sudden, in the middle of my message, a young teenage boy came down the aisle. He came up to me and confessed his addiction to pornography. I had not even given the altar call yet.

Then young people, one by one, started coming to the altar to repent of their sins. Our worship leader began to sing as I, along with other leaders, started ministering to these broken young people. Many decisions for Christ were made that day. It started to rain and many of the students went out from under the tent to get on their knees in the rain and worship Jesus. It was a major move of God.

As all of this was taking place, I thought of the Bible Man mask. The Lord moved that day upon the students to take off their mask of phoniness and confess their sins openly. The Bible says in II Tim. 3:5, *"Having a form of Godliness, but denying the power thereof: from such turn away."*

The word "form" in the Greek is "morphosis" and it means "an image or impression, an outward semblance." It means basically "an appearance." The word picture is a mask where the person appears to be one way but is actually another way under the mask. That day at the Christian festival, God removed the masks as students confessed their sins and repented.

You can see now how powerful the gift of Discerning of Spirits is. It gives you supernatural ability to see into the spiritual world. This gift is extremely necessary in this day and age. It can function as a form of protection from the influence of the enemy and from problems within the fellowship of believers. Sometimes individuals are involved within local fellowships that have the wrong kind of spirit.[3]

The gift of Discerning of Spirits is also needed when individuals are operating in other gifts of the Spirit. The Bible says, *"Let the prophets speak two or three, and let the other judge"* (I Cor. 14:29). A person operating in the gift of Discerning of Spirits would be helpful in judging prophecy. Is a particular prophecy of God, of man, or of the devil? Obviously, biblical discernment is needed to know if what is being spoken is scriptural or not.

Testing the Spirits

The Bible tells us to not believe every spirit, but we are to try the spirits to see if they are from God or not (I John 4:1). We are told that there are many false prophets who have gone out into the world so we must use discernment. We must understand that behind every teaching there is a spirit. It is either the Spirit of God, the Spirit of man or the Spirit of Antichrist. How does one "test the spirits" to discern which one it is? The Bible gives us the answer to this question in I John 4:3:

> *"And every spirit that confesseth not that Jesus Christ is come in the flesh is not of God: and this is that spirit of antichrist, whereof you have heard that it should come; and even now already is it in the world."*

If a teacher of the Word denies the incarnation of Jesus Christ (God in the flesh), then he is of the antichrist spirit. The fact that Jesus, being God, came in the form of man is vital to the work of atonement which He came to do. The incarnation speaks of the Cross and any preacher who does not preach the Cross or put emphasis on the Cross is of another spirit. This is most serious and must not be ignored by the Church or the believer.

When Christ was born (which is the incarnation), the angel proclaimed, *"Fear not: for, behold, I bring you good tidings of great joy, which shall be to all people. For unto you is born this day in the city of David, a Saviour, which is Christ the Lord"* (Luke 2:10-11).

We see from this verse that the incarnation is directly connected to the Cross of Christ. Emmanuel, God with us, came in the form of man for one reason: to die on a cruel cross to save us from our sins.

In this world, with so many spiritual needs and with such intensified spiritual activity, the gift of Discerning of Spirits is crucial. It is now being used and experienced more than at perhaps any other time in history.[4]

There are many deceived Christians today who believe that something is of God when it is really of the devil. One must remember that the devil can appear as an angel of light.

A short time ago, there was an evangelist who was brought into a church in Florida and many were claiming that God was birthing a revival. Many were claiming healing and all kinds of supernatural occurrences. There were millions of people watching these services night after night through the internet. Christians were flying in from all over the world to take part in these meetings. I was anxious to see if this was a true move of God, but as I viewed the services over the internet I knew right away that the man leading the revival was not of God. I immediately took a stand against these meetings and there were some who didn't like my position.

They asked me why I did not think it was of God. I told them it was because I listened to what this man was saying and he was not preaching or emphasizing the Cross. In fact, he was preaching false doctrine. My biblical discernment told me that he was not of the Holy Spirit. But the gift of Discerning of Spirits showed me the man was not right as well. To be honest, it seemed so obvious that I could not understand why so many were being deceived.

Shortly thereafter, the man's sin was revealed and the "so called" revival was over. But the most alarming part of the whole movement was how many pastors and leaders across the country could not discern the false doctrine or the false way. Any preacher not preaching, emphasizing, or explaining the Message of the Cross is preaching another Jesus and he is of another spirit (II Cor. 11:3-4).

Jesus discerned the spirit of Judas before Judas ever betrayed Him. On the night of the betrayal Jesus said to His disciples, *"But behold, the hand of him who betrayeth me is with me on the table"* (Luke 22:21). Jesus, operating in the gift of Discerning of Spirits, was able to recognize who was truly with Him and who was not.

The gift of Discerning of Spirits is often necessary in divine healing as well, as it can be a demon spirit that must be cast out before the person can be healed. Now you know why Paul said, "desire spiritual gifts," because they are so necessary in order to combat the forces of evil that come against us. Now we know why Paul did not want the body of Christ to be ignorant of spiritual gifts (I Cor. 12:1).

Chapter 9

THE POWER GIFTS

Gift of Faith

Now we enter into the second category of the gifts of the Spirit called the "Power Gifts."

The gift of Faith is a supernatural gift that is given to glorify Christ. Jesus, as with all the gifts, operated in this gift all the time. The Holy Spirit is His Spirit.

This gift is not talking about the normal faith to believe in Jesus to be saved, which every believer in Christ possesses. But the gift of "Faith" is an extra measure of faith given to believe for a miracle.

It is interesting that the gift of Faith precedes the gifts of Healing in the list found in I Corinthians 12:9. I don't believe this is an accident because you need the gift of Faith operating in your life for the gifts of Healing to manifest through you. The Word of God says that if you ask God for something and you don't have the faith to believe for it, then you should not expect to get it (James 1:5-7).

We see in the ministry of Jesus that He operated in faith before every miracle happened. Obviously, to walk on water you have to believe you can or else you would never step out of the boat.

Jesus taught his disciples how to operate in faith in Matthew 21 when he came to the fig tree. The Bible says He was hungry and when He looked at the fig tree He saw nothing; there was no fruit. He then said these words, *"Let no fruit grow on thee henceforward for ever"* (Matt. 21:19). And the Bible says that the fig tree withered away.

When the disciples saw it, they were amazed at how quickly it withered. Jesus said to them, *"Verily I say unto you, If ye have faith, and doubt not, ye shall not only do this which is done to the fig tree, but also if ye shall say unto this mountain, Be thou removed, and be thou cast into the sea; it shall be done"* (Matt. 21:21).

I remember one morning I woke up and looked in the mirror and I saw a small growth of skin forming on my upper lip. It was a strange sight and I was a little concerned by its presence. In the days and months that followed it grew a little larger and became very visible. I was a little self conscious of it but no matter what I did, still it remained on my lip.

One day I read this passage in scripture of Jesus speaking to the tree and telling it to wither. I thought to myself, how can I ask God to heal people with major abnormalities and sicknesses if I cannot even believe God to remove a small piece of skin from my upper lip? I then placed my finger over the skin growth and said these words, "In the name of Jesus, I command you to dry up and wither away."

Later that day, I looked in the mirror and it appeared to me that the skin growth was drying up and even shrinking. The following day, I wiped my face and a part of the skin growth came off. The next day, I was washing my face and when I dried it with a towel, the rest of the skin growth came right off. That piece of skin was on my upper lip for over six months, but now it is gone. It truly built my faith to believe God for the mountains to be removed as well.

The gift of Faith is given by God in order for us to operate in the supernatural power of the Holy Spirit. This is because faith is the prerequisite of God in order to see the power of the

Holy Spirit. Over and over in scripture, when Jesus healed someone He would say, "according to your faith, be it done unto you." He said in Matthew 21:22, *"And all things, whatsoever ye shall ask in prayer, believing, ye shall receive."* Notice "believing" is the precondition of receiving from God.

Gifts of Healing

Another one of the "Power Gifts" of the Spirit is the gifts of Healing. When the gifts of Healing are in operation, great and dramatic healings take place. We are commanded in the Word of God to pray for the sick. James 5:14-15 says, *"Is any sick among you? Let him call for the elders of the church; and let them prayer over him, anointing him with oil in the name of the Lord. And the prayer of faith shall save the sick, and the Lord shall raise him up;"*

We are commanded in the Word to pray for the sick and believe for their healing. So why is most of the modern Church not doing this? Why don't we see this every week in our church services?

It is no coincidence that the gifts of Healing are preceded by the gift of Faith as previously stated. The sad truth is that most today in the Church lack faith to believe for the sick to be healed. Even in Jesus' hometown, very few sick folks were healed because of unbelief (Mark 6:5-6). But, when the gift of Faith is present, the Spirit, many times, will anoint His servants with the gifts of Healing. Notice that it is the *gifts* of Healing and not the *gift* of Healing. Why is it in the plural and not in the singular?

I have heard it said by many biblical experts that they believe this is because there are many different sicknesses and therefore God gives certain individuals a specific anointing to heal certain kinds of sicknesses. I don't know if this is true, but I do believe God will give a person the specific faith for a specific sickness to be healed. For example, if God calls me to pray for a person who has a growth on their upper lip, I have great faith to see that growth removed because I have personally experienced it. Someone who has been healed out of a wheelchair will have great faith to see others in wheelchairs get up and be healed.

I have a friend named Marlene who was healed at the age of 19 of cerebral palsy. She once told me, "Mike, don't ever separate healing and evangelism, they go together." I want you to know that when someone who had been restricted to a wheelchair because of cerebral palsy is miraculously healed and tells you something about healing, you listen very carefully!

There was a crippled man in the Bible who was sitting at the Temple gate begging for money. When Peter and John came to the Temple to pray, they noticed the man as he held out his hand expecting to receive money from them, and Peter said to the man, *"Silver and gold have I none; but such as I have give I thee: In the name of Jesus Christ of Nazareth rise up and walk"* (Acts 3:6).

The Bible says that the man got up, was healed and went into the Temple with Peter and John walking and leaping and praising God. But the miracle doesn't stop there. The news of the miracle of this lame man walking spread throughout the city. The Bible says that because of this one miracle of healing, thousands of people came together and listened to Peter preach about the one, Jesus Christ, who had healed this man and 5,000 people were saved (Acts 4:4). This is exactly what Marlene meant: don't ever separate healing and evangelism. Divine healing is the greatest tool of evangelism.

The modern Church that has denied the power of the Holy Spirit, and says the gifts of the Spirit are not for today, does not see many people being healed. But if the Church will come back to the Word of God and believe that Jesus Christ is the same yesterday, and today, and forever (Hebrews 13:8), then the gifts of the Spirit will be restored. They will begin to see the moving and operation of the Holy Spirit. If God starts moving in the area of divine healing, we will see thousands coming to Christ. Now you know why Paul said, *"desire spiritual gifts."*

Any preacher who teaches that the gifts of the Spirit are not for today, or who simply ignores the teaching of the gifts of the Spirit, will be accountable one day for limiting God and for not believing in His whole counsel. This may be blunt, but I believe it to be true. Also I believe church or preacher who does not believe the gifts of the Spirit are for today falls under the same classification in which Jesus put the Laodicean Church. He called them "lukewarm" and as such would spit them out of His mouth (Rev. 3:16).

The Laodicean Church was rich, but they had no power, just like the modern Church today. The Lord instructed the Laodicean Church to anoint their eyes with eye salve (which Laodicea produced and made a lot of money from) so they could see clearly. In other words, they needed to be healed spiritually so that they could see where they were lacking. Jesus said to this church, *"As many as I love, I rebuke and chasten: be zealous therefore, and repent"* (Rev. 3:19). If only the Church of today would heed this command of Jesus!

When I first began in ministry, the Lord taught me a valuable lesson in the area of divine healing. My mother was very sick and had been bleeding for 21 days. It was Sunday and I went to church and then was invited to go out on a boat with a family from the church. I spent the whole day with them. When I came home my father lit into me about being so concerned with my own life that I was being insensitive to my mom's condition. I could tell that Dad was very concerned about Mom. He really let me have it and, even though I was very defensive, inside my heart I knew he was right.

Mom had become so weak she could not even get out of bed and I didn't even call the entire day to see how she was doing. Even worse, in all the 21 days I never stopped to pray for her. I guess I just thought it would pass and she would get better. However she wasn't getting better, she was getting weaker.

After Dad finished yelling at me, all of sudden I felt deep pains begin in my stomach. The pains got so severe that I could hardly make it to my bedroom. I laid there in my bed yelling out in pain. My mother came into my room from her sickbed and rubbed my back as I laid there in pain. I then just about crawled to the bathroom, hoping that whatever was in me would come out. I yelled out over the sink, "In the name of Jesus come out." After the third time my deliverance came. I got sick and made a complete mess of the bathroom. I remember being so weak that I didn't have the strength to clean it up. I just crawled back into my bed, hoping to clean it up later. I soon fell into a deep sleep and the next thing I knew it was morning.

I got up and found that the bathroom had been cleaned. Mom was in bed sleeping and I asked Dad who cleaned up the bathroom. He said, "Your mother got down on her hands and knees and did it." I was so convicted. A short time later that morning, I felt the Spirit of God speak to my heart through His Word for Mom's healing. The gift of Faith immediately came over me for her to be healed. I went into her room and read one of the Psalms to her on healing. I then laid my hands on her and prayed that God would touch her.

After praying for her, I had to go out. I came home later that afternoon only to find her up and cooking dinner, something she hadn't been able to do in days. She said, "Mike, right after you prayed I started to feel strength come back in my body and the bleeding ceased. I feel fine now."

We serve a miracle-working God, but in order for Him to work, faith must be present first. His Word says, *"But without faith it is impossible to please him"* (Hebrews 11:6).

Many ask the question, "why are some people are healed and others are not healed?" Remember, the gifts of Healing operate as the Lord wills and not as man wills (I Cor. 12:11). I cannot answer this question completely. There are many reasons why people may not receive healing from God. Sometimes it is obvious and sometimes it is not. Unless God gives you a Word of Knowledge or Wisdom, you may not know the answer until you get to heaven. But one thing we do know, based on the Word of God, the Lord wants to heal and is more than able. We are to pray for the sick and continue to believe for miracles.

Untold millions have been healed by God in supernatural ways, and the Holy Spirit still works through compassionate human beings who know God, are filled with His Spirit and believe for the impossible. If you are sick in body, keep on believing for your healing. The Bible teaches us to be persistent in our asking, seeking and knocking (Luke 11:10) and, by all means, make sure you attend a church that believes divine healing is included in the work of the Cross and regularly prays for the sick.

The Working of Miracles

First, let's define what the word "miracle" means. The Webster Dictionary defines it as "an extraordinary event manifesting divine intervention in human affairs." The word in the Greek language for "miracle" is "dunamis" which means "power, inherent ability, is used of a supernatural origin and character, such as could not be produced by natural agents and means."[1]

The "Working of Miracles" includes anything that God does that man can't do. This is what we call a miracle. Obviously, divine healing falls into this classification, but it also includes miracles even beyond physical healing.

There were miracles other than divine healing in the Old Testament such as:

- Sarah having a child at the age of 90 years old (Gen. 21)

- The parting of the Red Sea (Ex. 14:21-31)

- The fire falling on Mount Carmel through the prayer of the Prophet Elijah (I Kings 18)

- The sun standing still for 24 hours for Joshua (Josh.10:12-14)

- The multiplication of the widow's oil (II Kings 4)

- And many more!

Jesus operated in the gift of Miracles when He walked on water to the disciples' boat and then called Peter out on the waters (Matt. 14:29), when He told the disciples to go and they would find a shekel in the mouth of a fish in order to pay the tax of Caesar (Matt. 17:24 - 27), when He turned the water into wine (John 2), when He fed the 5,000 people with two loaves and five fish (Luke 9:10-17), etc.

The gift of Miracles is always to bring glory to God, help meet people's needs and build faith.

Jesus said that these signs would follow those who believe: *"In My name shall they cast out devils; they shall speak with new tongues; They shall take up serpents; and if they drink any deadly thing, it shall not hurt them; they shall lay hands on the sick, and they shall recover."* (Mark 16:17-18). Every one of these things takes a miracle of God to happen.

The miracles of Jesus were so amazing, the mind cannot really comprehend them. But Jesus said, *"Verily, verily, I say unto you, He who believes on me, the works that I do shall he do also; and greater works than these shall he do; because I go unto my Father"* (John 14:12). Here Jesus is not saying that the works that the Church will do will be greater than what

He did in quality, but in quantity because His Holy Spirit can be working everywhere in the world at the same time.

What are miracles meant to do? The main intention or purpose of miracles is to prove the validity of who Jesus is. When John the Baptist was in prison, he began to question in his own mind whether or not Jesus really was the Christ. I am sure the loneliness, isolation and despair of being soon martyred was causing him to doubt what he had already announced publicly (John 1:29). He sent two of his disciples to question Jesus if He, in fact, was the Messiah or if they should look for another. Jesus said to them: *"Go and show John again those things which you do hear and see: The blind receive their sight, and the lame walk, the lepers are cleansed, and the deaf hear, and the dead are raised up, and the poor have the gospel preached to them"* (Matt. 11:4-5).

It is the Gospel preached (the Message of the Cross), and the miracles of God that follow that help you to know it is of God. Paul said in I Cor. 2:4-5, *"And my speech and my preaching was not with enticing words of man's wisdom, but in demonstration of the Spirit and of power: That your faith should not stand in the wisdom of men, but in the power of God."*

To have the Word only and not the power of God is not a full Gospel presentation. The Word with power is how the early Church experienced God and it is not the intention of God to ever change that plan. The miracles of God are still flowing today to whosoever will believe. For Jesus said, *"all things are possible to him who believeth"* (Mark 9:23).

I once had a pastor of a very large church take issue with me over me taking my son to the altar for healing prayer. It was witnessed by over 5,000 young people. This particular pastor had a problem with it because he was concerned about what would happen to the faith of those young people since they had prayed, but my son wasn't healed. I respectfully said to him that I didn't think it was my responsibility to protect

God's reputation. I told him I believed God was big enough to do that all by Himself. My job is only to believe what the Word of God says and leave the rest up to Him. I then asked this pastor if he believed God could heal my son (of his crippling disease), and he said, "I believe He can, but I don't believe He will." And then he said, "But I hope you prove me wrong!"

True faith in miracles for today doesn't just believe that God can, but it also believes He will. The Bible defines faith in Hebrews 11:1, "*Now faith is the substance of things hoped for, the evidence of things not seen.*" Someone with true faith has the evidence in his heart before he even sees the miracle.

Several years ago, the Make-a-Wish Foundation sent our son Matthew, and our whole family on an all-expense-paid trip to Disney World to make Matthew's wish come true. We had one of the best times our family has ever had. There were several times on the trip that the presence of God came over me as I watched how much fun our son Matthew was having, even though he was restricted to a wheelchair.

As we were leaving the Orlando airport to board the plane to come home, the ticket counter attendant at the gate approached me and asked me if they could be of special assistance to Matthew in getting his wheelchair and him on the plane. I said that would be very helpful. I thanked her for her kindness. She had really made us feel special.

Our whole family boarded the plane and Matthew was buckled in his seat. We were sitting and waiting for the crew to close the hatch of the plane and take off. Then, all of a sudden, this kind lady from the ticket counter boarded the plane and came down the aisle. She looked me straight in the eye and said these words, "Sir, I just had to come on this plane and tell you that your father is one of the most loving and kind men that I have ever met." My wife and I were totally confused by her statement since my father was back in Buffalo, where he lives with my mom. So, I asked her what he said to her. She said, "Your dad came up to me and my assistant at the counter and said, 'Ma'am, I want to thank you for taking such good care of my grandson, it means so much to me.'" She told me that when he spoke those words, she never, in all of her life, felt so much love come over her. She and her assistant both started crying.

I then began to discern what had happened and I asked her, "What did he look like and what was he wearing?" She said, "He had white hair, blue eyes and he was in jeans and a denim shirt." I told her that my father has dark hair and hazel eyes and he lives in Buffalo, New York. I then asked one more question, "Did you see which way he went?" Her answer confirmed my suspicion. She said, "That's the craziest thing of all. When he made us cry my assistant said to me, 'You have to get this man to fill out a customer service card,' so I reached down to get one from under the counter and when I looked up, he was gone." She said they looked all around, but it was as if he had vanished. She said they looked in both directions and he was no where to be found.

I looked at the dear lady and I said, "Ma'am, what is your name?" She said her name was Rachel. I said, "Rachel, you just saw an angel. The Bible says that when we show hospitality to strangers, we sometimes entertain angels unaware." (Hebrews 11:2).

She stared right through me for a moment as she contemplated what I had just said. Tears formed in her eyes and then all of sudden she snapped out of her momentary trance, looked back at me and said, "Sir, I've got to go," and she turned around and walked off the plane as they closed the hatch.

The presence of God at that moment came over me and I began to witness to all the people sitting around us on the plane who had been listening to the conversation. My sister Linda, who came on the trip to be our children's nanny, was so overwhelmed by what she had just heard, that she had chill bumps on her arm for almost 10 minutes.

My brothers and sisters, we serve a God of miracles and He will perform miracles all around us if only we believe. The gift of Miracles is still in operation today as the Spirit wills (ICor. 12:11).

One word of caution here is that any miracle must always be centered on the preaching of Jesus Christ and the Cross. If the Gospel message is not being preached, no matter what the manifestations are, one should avoid the teacher, church or movement. Remember that the Antichrist will one day come with great signs and lying wonders (2 Thess. 2:9-10).

Chapter 10

THE VOCAL GIFTS

Gift of Prophecy

The third category of Spiritual Gifts is "Vocal Gifts" or "Inspiration Gifts." They are gifts that "say" something. The first one is the gift of Prophecy. The word "prophecy" in the Hebrew means "to flow forth." It also carries with it the thought "to bubble forth like a fountain, to let drop, to lift up, to tumble forth, and to spring forth." The Greek word that is translated "prophecy" means "to speak for another."[1]

In the Old Testament, prophecy is mainly foretelling, (which means to predict future events), and in the New Testament prophecy is mainly forth-telling, (which means to give a word to someone from God to encourage them). Prophecy is supernatural speech in a known language. The Bible makes significance of this gift more so than any of the other gifts. The Scriptures say "covet to prophesy" (I Cor 14:39).

The Bible tells us in I Cor. 12 that Prophecy is for three main things:

1) Edification – To build up

2) Exhortation – To urge on or encourage

3) Comfort – For consolation

Prophecy is not preaching, however sometimes there can be an element of prophecy in a sermon. Preachers may all of a sudden speak prophetically in their sermons and may not even know it, but will be speaking right to a person's need or situation. Inspired preaching is not the gift of Prophecy. The gift of Prophecy is when the Spirit of God wants to speak a specific message to an individual or group of people.

In the New Testament, this gift is not normally used to forecast doom, judgment or condemnation. It is primarily used for edification, exhortation and comfort. The Bible says that when prophecy is given it is to be proved or, in other words, tested to make sure it is from God (I Thes. 5:20-21).

There is a lot of abuse of this gift today. Christians have not followed the scriptures to "prove" the prophecy that is given, which means to go to the scriptures and go to the Lord for confirmation on what has been said. Many have taken a so called "word" from God (which is actually not of God) and have left their jobs, sold their homes, etc. based on the prophetic word that was spoken. This has caused great pain and suffering and many have even become disenchanted with God because the "prophetic word" spoken over them did not turn out correct.

I was in a service in Rochester, NY and a preacher called me out of the crowd and gave a prophetic word over me. At the time it was a great encouragement to me. The church even sent me to its bookstore after the service to get the prophetic word that was spoken over me on tape.

All of this was fine except for one thing: what the preacher said never came true and actually the opposite happened. Obviously, this preacher did not hear correctly from the Lord. That is why every prophecy must be judged.

There is a movement out there called "the Prophetic Movement" but most of it would fall under the classification of "the Pathetic Movement" because it is mainly men and women running around speaking to large crowds of people and telling them what they want to hear. These leaders are deceived and misled. How do I know that? Because they are not preaching the Gospel, nor do they place an emphasis on the Cross. The emphasis is on their "prophetic gifting."

There are many churches today that bring in these so-called prophets and, after they preach, they line the people up at the altar so the prophet can prophesy over them. Now, God does move in the prophetic to speak to His people but every prophecy should be judged. How does one do that?

It should be judged by two or three witnesses: *"at the mouth of two witnesses, or at the mouth of three witnesses, shall the matter be established"* (Deut. 19:15). A person should never alter the course of his life based upon one person professing to prophesy. He should always have a confirmation in his own heart that this is exactly what God is speaking. As well, it should always line up with scripture.

I remember when I first graduated from college and I was seeking God as to what profession I should go into: teaching or full-time youth ministry. I went to North Carolina on a week-long vacation to seek God about my future. I prayed and fasted for God to speak to me. I didn't hear Him say a word to me about my future. I went home a little discouraged to say the least. But in the following week after I returned home, I had three different individuals, whom I had never met before, come up to me randomly and ask me if I was in youth ministry. I would ask them "why do you ask me that?" All three said the same thing, "You just look like someone who should be in youth ministry."

God used those three individuals to confirm what I already sensed in my heart. As a result, I joined the ministry of Youth For Christ and I worked with them for over 17 years. It was the right decision because it was God's will for my life.

The gift of Prophecy is an amazing gift and it is to be used to build faith and confirm the Lord's direction in one's life. It is used to edify and exhort the believer in Christ. The Bible says:

"But he who prophesieth speaketh unto men to edification (to build up), *and exhortation, and comfort"* (I Cor. 14:3).

In Revelation 19:10 the Bible says, *"And I fell at his feet to worship him. And he said unto me, See thou do it not: I am thy fellowservant, and of thy brethren that have the testimony of Jesus: worship God: for the testimony of Jesus is the Spirit of prophecy."* The testimony of Jesus is the Spirit of prophecy. This means that all prophecy in one way or another should be centered around lifting up Jesus Christ and what He did on the Cross to save us. The gift is never to be used to puff up man, but only to bring people to Christ.

The gift of Prophecy is to encourage and edify the Church (ICor. 14:5). Also, the gift of Prophecy can be used to uncover the secrets of man's heart and convict the unbeliever of sins and cause him or her to know that God is real (I Cor. 14:24-25).

There is much zeal in the Church today for the gift of Prophecy, but the scriptures give us the order of this gift for public services. It says that during the course of a service, the Prophets should only speak two or three and their prophecies should be judged (I Cor. 14:29).

Divers Kinds of Tongues and
Interpretation of Tongues

Another gift under the "Vocal Gift" category is the speaking in other tongues. There are many different languages in the world today, due to the scattering of the languages at the tower of Babel (Gen. 11).

We have a language barrier today which causes difficulties to say the least. I remember when I was traveling home from a mission's trip in Brazil, I was at the airport and I couldn't find my gate. Not knowing Portuguese, I was frantically trying to find someone who spoke English and could help me before I missed my flight. Praise God, I finally found someone who was able to help me or else I might still be there. So, the scattering of the languages by God, due to man's sin, has caused great difficulties in the world.

However, the Holy Spirit, who gives help to man, has given the gift of "Divers (various) Kinds of Tongues" to bring in not man's unity, but the Spirit's unity (Eph. 4:3).

Tongues can be used in two ways:
1) A Devotional Prayer life with God
2) A Ministry gift to bring God's message to His Church

Let's look first at the devotional use of speaking in other tongues. Private devotional tongues are for prayer (speaking in tongues) and worship (singing in tongues) as they are given for communication unto God. The Bible says:

"What is it then? I will pray with the spirit, and I will pray with the understanding also (pray in your native language*): I will sing with the spirit, and I will sing with the understanding also"* (I Cor. 14:15).

This does not require interpretation because it is speaking to God and not to man. When the speaking with other tongues is used in one's devotional life, either in prayer or singing in the Spirit, this is not the gift of Tongues.

The gift of Tongues is when one speaks a message to the congregation and there is interpretation for the people to understand what is being said. When there is no interpretation, then the gift of Tongues should not be used. Why? Because no one can be helped as no one understands what is being said.

In the Corinthian Church, people were speaking in other tongues out loud and there was no interpretation being given, and so there was confusion due to the fact that no one understood what was being said. This seems to be an obvious conclusion. Why would I want to speak out loud to be heard if no one can understand me? However, there were some in the early (and the modern) Church who liked to flex their spiritual gifts in front of man. Why did Paul say not to do it? Because it is meaningless without the gift of Interpretation (I Cor. 14:9). There is no teaching value to speaking in tongues unless there is an interpreter present (I Cor. 14:19), and it is childish to do so (I Cor. 14:20). Also, it makes the unbeliever (non Christian) and the unlearned (someone who is not yet baptized with the Holy Spirit) think you have lost your mind and are crazy (I Cor. 14:23). Speaking in tongues with no interpretation doesn't edify anyone but the speaker (I Cor.14:3, 26).

If you do have an interpreter present in a service, then, as with the gift of Prophecy, it should be limited to two or three messages per service. But again there must be someone who has the gift of Interpretation present for the gift of Tongues to be in operation in a public service. Like the gift of Prophecy, the gift of Tongues, when it is accompanied with the gift of Interpretation, is a great blessing to the congregation and it will edify and build up the Church.

When the Holy Spirit comes upon a person to speak in tongues in a gathering, He will at times give the interpretation to the same one who gave the message in tongues. This is completely in order and many times God will do it in this fashion and other times he will use two people, one to give the message in tongues and one to give the interpretation.

A friend of mine once told me a story of when he was called to the former Soviet Union to preach at a fairly large church. He could not speak a word of Russian so he had to preach through an interpreter. The day before he was to preach in this Russian church, the pastor of that church introduced him to the person who was going to interpret his message. In the course of their time together, this preacher asked the dear lady (who was his assigned interpreter) if she believed in the gift of speaking in other Tongues. The woman said that she was of a Baptist persuasion and believed that the gifts of the Spirit had ceased when the early Church closed the canon of scripture (i.e. the Bible). My friend tried to persuade her that the Lord still worked through the nine gifts of the Spirit, but he could tell she was not convinced.

The next day, as my friend was preaching his message in English and she was interpreting the message in Russian for the people, all of sudden in the middle of his message the Holy Spirit came upon him. He began to speak in another tongue. He told me he never experienced anything like this before and it was the first time he had ever broken into tongues publicly in the middle of preaching.

He quickly realized that he actually was speaking Russian even though he had never learned the language. The people in the church began to respond to his message with joy, and even though he didn't understand, he knew the Spirit was moving strongly. He said he glanced over to his interpreter who knew he could not speak Russian and she was standing there with tears rolling down her cheeks. That dear lady had to change her theology that day and admit that God is still working through the gifts of the Spirit just as He had done in the Book of Acts. Oh, Praise God!

The gifts of the Spirit are precious, perfect and given for God's glory to accomplish His purposes. Who are we to say no to them? I can't heal the sick, raise the dead, part the Red Sea, etc., but God can and does as He wills. He still chooses to use His people to move in the power of His Holy Spirit in miraculous ways. I'm open, I'm willing. Are You? If you want to be all that God has created you to be and to be used in every way He wills, then tell Him. Yes, even right now!

Chapter 11

THE "CONTROVERSY"

The question must be asked, why have the gifts of the Holy Spirit been so controversial and caused so much confusion and disunity in the body of Christ? First of all, understand that God is not the author of confusion. The Bible says, *"For God is not the author of confusion, but of peace, as in all churches of the saints"* (I Corinthians 14:33).

Interestingly enough, this verse is found right after the Holy Spirit (through Paul) has written three chapters on spiritual gifts and their proper use. So, there was obviously confusion in the early Church over the gifts of the Spirit and, through the Apostle Paul, God gave a detailed explanation to clear up the confusion. So why is there still today (2,000 years later) confusion over the use of spiritual gifts? There are three main reasons:

The Church does not follow the instructions laid out in detail in scripture regarding the use of spiritual gifts in the church.

The Church chooses not to believe that I Corinthians 12-14 applies to the modern day Church (a very dangerous assumption by the way).

The Church adds to the scriptures, following its own personal direction and not the direction the Holy Spirit has laid out in scripture.

If the Church doesn't follow what the scriptures say, then it will be led to a state of confusion when it comes to speaking in other tongues or any other spiritual gift for that matter. The Bible must not be changed in either direction, taking away from it or adding to it. The Bible must not be tampered with; it must only be believed. Any Christian who follows a particular preacher from any church or denomination who does not believe and follow the complete Word of God is heading into spiritual problems.

Our only source of spiritual truth is the Word of God and it is only the Word of God that defines our spiritual experience. Our experience doesn't define the Bible; the Bible defines our experience. We must clearly understand this.

If someone in the Church has an experience that cannot be substantiated by the Word of God, then that person should keep that experience to themselves. They should not teach it as something that should be duplicated by others. If someone introduces a new concept or experience that you are not familiar with, the question must be asked, "Do you have Bible for that?" If the answer is no, then that teaching, concept or personal experience should go no further – to do so can be very dangerous.

However, if someone's experience or teaching is consistent with the Word of God, then it should be accepted and sought after if the Bible encourages such duplication. Let me give you an example.

A person experiences the power of God come over him and he begins to speak in another tongue (an unlearned language). This experience is very consistent with the New Testament and the early Church found in the Book of Acts (Acts 2:4,10:44-6 and 19:1-6). Therefore, we can accept this as a legitimate experience from God and one that can be sought after for duplication in one's own life, for even Paul said, *"I would that ye all spake with tongues"* (I Cor. 14:5).

The problems begin when a preacher says that "speaking in tongues is not for today." This is a belief in many circles of the modern Church that brings confusion into the Body of Christ. Where does this belief stem from?

First of all, the belief that speaking in tongues is not for today is mostly, if not always, taught by preachers and teachers who have not personally received the Baptism with the Holy Spirit with the evidence of speaking with other tongues. So, they are simply speaking from their intellect and not spiritual revelation. Just as before someone is saved, it is very difficult for them to understand justification by faith. When they are saved and born again, however, it makes all the sense in the world. Why? Because they have experienced it in their own lives.

Has Speaking in Tongues Ceased?

Some teach today, in mainline churches, that the gift of Tongues "ceased" (stopped) when the Bible was completed. The verse that they use is I Cor. 13:8 which says, *"Charity never faileth: but whether there be prophecies, they shall fail; whether there be tongues, they shall cease; whether there be knowledge, it shall vanish away."*

The Bible student should notice something that is troubling. If this verse is saying that "tongues has ceased" today, then you also must conclude that "prophecies" have been done away with and "knowledge" has vanished away. Interestingly enough, we are living today in the most advanced society in the history of the world. Knowledge is advancing faster than at any other time in the history of man and, when it comes to prophecy, we are literally seeing, in our day, prophecies being fulfilled, especially as it concerns the Nation of Israel.

So, one can only conclude in the context of this verse that if knowledge is not vanishing and prophecy is not fading, then neither is speaking in tongues. This is confirmed by millions of people who have been baptized with the Holy Spirit and have received the gift of Tongues as the initial evidence. Rapid increase began in 1906 at the Azusa Street Revival in Los Angeles, and it has continued to gain momentum ever since.

In fact, the Bible prophesies in Joel 2:28-29 that there will be a great outpouring of the Holy Spirit in the last days. On the Day of Pentecost, Peter, when describing why the Jews were speaking in other languages, said, *"This is that which was spoken by the prophet Joel"* (Acts 2:16). So, if they were speaking in tongues in the Book of Acts on the Day of Pentecost and beyond, and they are going to be speaking in tongues in the last days prior to the great and terrible day of the Lord (Joel 2:31), then one can conclude that tongues has not ceased, and is not going to cease, in this dispensation.

The Bible does tell us when tongues will cease, and when knowledge shall vanish away and prophecy will fail (be done away). The Bible says two verses later, *"But when that which is perfect is come, then that which is in part shall be done away"* (ICor. 13:10).

Notice the word in I Corinthians 13:10, "perfect." The Greek word is "Teleios" and it means "goal, purpose, adult, full-grown, of full age, as opposite to little children." The "teleios is one who has obtained his moral end, the goal for which he was intended, namely, to be a man obedient in Christ."[1]

Obviously, the Christian man has not reached his moral end until he meets Christ, "the Perfect one." The Bible says, *"Being confident of this very thing, that he which hath begun a good work in you will perform it until the day of Jesus Christ"* (Phil. 1:6). So, until the day of Christ we are still a work in progress. Jesus Christ is the "Perfect One" and when the "Perfect" comes (which is the Day of Christ), we will not need knowledge for we will see Him as He is. At that moment, prophecy will no longer be needed because we will have Christ personally to teach us all things and we will not need to speak in tongues as we will speak directly to Him, face to face.

A Closed Canon

Those that hold to the teaching that "tongues have ceased" say that when the "closed canon of scripture" (the Bible) was given to man, the gifts of the Spirit were no longer needed. They say that the gifts of the Spirit were only for the early Church and when the last apostle died, the gifts are no longer in operation because the Word of God is now available.

This teaching has no scriptural basis and has caused more damage in the personal growth of the Church than I believe any other teaching has. It has caused believers to walk in defeat and has quenched the power of the Holy Spirit in many churches, and even entire denominations. It has also caused division in the Body of Christ and has split the Church down the middle.

Now, there are many problems with this teaching and many holes in this kind of logic. Mainly, if you believe in this teaching you will be left with the written Word, but you will see and experience very little of the living or active Word in your life.

A youth leader, who had been taught that the gifts of the Spirit had ceased, confronted me once. I made the statement that the Lord spoke to my heart and said, "I want you to take the Niagara Youth Conference (a ministry to young people that we had held for many years in Niagara Falls) city to city and I want you to build MY Church." He had an issue with me saying that the Lord had spoken to my heart and what I had said that God told me was not found in the Bible. In other words, he wanted chapter and verse for what I said the Lord spoke to me about.

I asked him, "Hasn't the Lord ever spoken to your heart directly?" He replied that the Lord speaks only through His Word. I said to him "Hasn't there ever been a thought in your heart like, you need to call your mother today, or some other word that, after you followed it, you were convinced it was the Lord who spoke it to your heart?" He looked back at me dumbfounded.

The Cessation Theory

When you take the stance that the gifts of the Spirit have ceased for today, in essence you are saying that there is no Word of Wisdom or Word of Knowledge from God to man, meaning God doesn't speak directly to man anymore. That means John 10:27, where Jesus said, *"My sheep hear my voice, and I know them, and they follow me,"* does not apply today because God doesn't speak except through His written Word (the Bible).

If you believe that the gifts of the Spirit have ceased for today, you are also saying that God does not give people a "special faith" for a particular situation in their life (I Corinthians 12:9). You are saying that God doesn't give man a special anointing to pray for the sick (i.e. gifts of Healing) because God doesn't use man to heal anymore. A cessation believer (one who believes the gifts have ceased) might say they believe God still heals today but He doesn't give man the gifts of Healing. So, in these churches you will not see James 5:14-16 being carried out which says: *"Is any sick among you? Let him call for the elders of the church; and let them pray over him, anointing him with oil in the name of the Lord: And the prayer of faith shall save the sick, and the lord shall raise him up; and if he have committed sins, they shall be forgiven him."*

Some years ago, my wife and I were vacationing in Florida and it was Sunday morning. I found an Assembly of God Church near our hotel and went to the service. There was a man there who preached (if I remember correctly) on divine healing and then he gave an altar call for those who were sick in body. I had been suffering with a back problem for some time and the problem caused circulation issues in my legs. I went up for prayer and the man laid hands on me and the Lord spoke a Word of Knowledge to him. He told me what was causing the back pain and then he prayed and the Lord touched me through this man's prayer and my back was healed. Praise God!

I know the Lord still moves in Words of Knowledge and divine healing and He still uses man to get His work done. But if a church believes that the gifts ceased at the close of the complete canon of scripture, then you will not see altar calls for healing. What a tragedy this is, and what a reproach this is to God Almighty and to His Word.

If a church believes that the gifts of the Spirit have ceased today, then you won't see "the Working of Miracles" in that Church. If a miracle does occur, it won't be reported or emphasized because the teaching says those things don't happen any more.

If you believe that the gifts have ceased in this dispensation, then verses like Mark 9:23, *"Jesus said unto him, If thou canst believe, all things are possible to him that believeth,"* don't apply for today because "all things" are not possible, at least in terms of God using man in the gifts of the Spirit.

If you believe in the cessation theory, then there are no "Words of Prophecy" for today other than the written Word of God. You are saying that God does not speak today other than His written Word. You are saying that God has said all He is going to say to man and for the past 1,900 years He has been silent other than the written Word of God. In that case, Jeremiah 33:3 is not for today which says, *"Call unto me, and I will answer thee, and show thee great and mighty things, which thou knowest not."* If the Word of Knowledge, Word of

Wisdom and Prophecy have ceased, then God will not answer you when you call except through the written Word of God.

Let me say, I am not demeaning the Word of God at all, God forbid! I can't remember how many times (it is probably in the thousands) that God has used His Word to speak to me. I have studied His Word endlessly, as every believer should. However, God is not limited to speaking to me only when my Bible is open. He will speak wherever and whenever He wills. Though the Lord can speak to us when we are not reading the Bible, He will never say anything that contradicts His Word. If it does, then you did not hear from God, you heard from someone else.

God still speaks today through the Word of Knowledge, the Word of Wisdom and Prophecy. To say that He doesn't cuts off the supernatural power of the Holy Spirit that makes our walk with Christ so personal and so amazing. Why would you ever want to believe that I Corinthians 12 is not for today?

Finally, if a Christian believes that the gifts of the Spirit have ceased, he will not believe that speaking with other Tongues and the Interpretation of Tongues are valid for today. Also, according to this teaching, every church and every Christian that exercise these gifts are babbling and deceived.

Look at the millions of Christians worldwide who claim to have the gift of Tongues and see the evidence of the nine gifts functioning today. Study the scriptures and see that the New Testament teaches the gifts of the Spirit without any scriptures that say that the gifts are going to cease before Jesus comes back. I believe you have to conclude that I Corinthians 12-14 is given for all believers for the entire dispensation of Grace, or what we call the Church Age.

The Inspired Word of God

If one believes that the gifts of the Spirit were only used for the time period before the Church had the completed Bible, why would God, the Holy Spirit, put all that teaching on the gifts of the Spirit in the Bible for us to learn when they were only going to be used for the early church and are no longer in effect today?

The Bible, or the closed canon of scripture, was completed when the last apostle died, who was John the beloved. It is believed that he died around the year 100 A.D. So if the gifts of the Spirit were no longer needed when the Bible was completed, then why would God include, in the writings of the New Testament, so much about the gifts? If the Lord intended for the gifts to cease, then what would be the purpose of inspiring Paul to write three chapters in Corinthians (I Cor. 12-14) on proper use of the gifts in the Church? Wouldn't this letter that Paul wrote be better only sent to the Corinthian Church and not given by God as one of the 66 Holy Spirit-inspired books of the Bible?

John ended his Gospel with the following words: *"And there are also many other things which Jesus did, the which, if they should be written every one, I suppose that even the world itself could not contain the books that should be written. Amen."* (John 21:25) So, the Lord has only given us partial knowledge in His Word. As it has been said, *"the half has never yet been told."* But what we do have is what He wants us to know right now.

So, my question for all the cessation believers is, why would the Lord inspire Paul to give us so much insight into the gifts of the Spirit if He was going to cause the gifts to cease in and around 100 AD? That logic says that this portion of scripture has no relevance for the Church of today and actually for the Church of the past 1,900 years. It doesn't make sense that it would be included and, add to the fact that there is evidence all over the world that the gifts are still in operation, one must come to the conclusion that the gifts of the Spirit are biblical and are still for today and those who are denying this are seriously mistaken.

The Bible says in Hebrews 13:8, *"Jesus Christ the same yesterday, and today, and forever."* The verse that follows provides a warning to us all, *"Be not carried about with divers and strange doctrines. For it is a good thing that the heart be established with grace; not with meats, which have not profited them that have been occupied therein"* (Hebrews 13:9). This verse is saying that anything that changes the faith with religious ceremonies is to be avoided. The Gospel of Christ, the Grace of God, must not be changed or diluted.

There is a serious warning to anyone who denies the full power of the Holy Spirit by saying or believing that the gifts of the Spirit or the Baptism with the Holy Spirit is not for today and it is, *"Having a form of godliness, but denying the power thereof: from such turn away"* (II Timothy 3:5).

Why "Tongues" is so Controversial

The gift of speaking in other tongues has really been the dividing line between Pentecostals/Charismatics and non-Charismatics. It has caused more division and more confusion than any of the other eight gifts. Why? Because, as with all of the gifts, the devil tries to prevent, confuse and counterfeit it. He knows that the power of God is released through this gift.

The Bible teaches us that when one is filled with the Holy Spirit, that person will speak in other tongues. Speaking with other tongues is the evidence that one is filled with the Holy Spirit. This doctrine is taken from a number of scriptures in the New Testament:

"And they were all filled with the Holy Ghost, and began to speak with <u>other tongues</u>, as the Spirit gave them utterance." (Acts 2:4)

"While Peter yet spake these words, the Holy Ghost fell on all them which heard the word. And they of the circumcision which believed were astonished, as many as came with Peter, because that on the gentiles also was poured out the gift of the Holy Ghost. For they heard them speak with tongues, and magnify God." (Acts 10:44-46)

"And when Paul laid his hands upon them, the Holy Ghost came on them; and they spake with tongues, and prophesied." (Acts 19:6)

Also, when Jesus was giving His disciples the great commission, He said these words:

"Go ye into all the world, and preach the gospel to every creature. He that believeth and is baptized shall be saved; but he that believeth not shall be damned. And these signs shall follow them who believe; In my name shall they cast out devils; they shall speak with new tongues; they shall take up serpents; and if they drink any deadly thing, it shall not hurt them; they shall lay hands on the sick, and they shall recover." (Mark 16:15-18)

So, here is the dividing line for many in the Body of Christ. A large segment of Christians believe these scriptures are saying that the speaking of tongues is for today and, not only that, but it is a sign that one has been filled with the Holy Spirit. In other words, if a believer in Christ does not speak with other tongues, they have not yet been baptized with the Holy Spirit. This is where the rub begins!

Many Christians who have not spoken in other tongues and do not believe it is a valid gift for today do not like being told or even thinking that one Christian has the infilling of the Spirit and they don't. They will take offense to this, as to think that the Christian who speaks in tongues thinks he is better or more spiritual than they are.

As well, there are Christians who have been so arrogant as to think they are more elite because they can speak in tongues or because they have some other gift and someone else doesn't. This is just spiritual pride and it is sin. Everything we receive from the Lord is because of grace, undeserved favor, so where is the boasting?

Several years ago, our ministry called for a two-day retreat where several leaders of major Christian organizations came together to discuss the Holy Spirit and what we believed about Him. Our organizations were working together to win young people to Christ and were producing youth conferences in other cities across America. We thought it was important that we all were in unity concerning our beliefs of the Person and workings of the Holy Spirit.

The meeting began with a question: what is your experience and your belief of how one is filled with the Holy Spirit? There were probably about 10-15 leaders in this meeting. As we went around the room it was amazing how many different thoughts and beliefs we had about the Holy Spirit.

When it came to my turn I shared my experience of how I was filled with the Holy Spirit at the University of Buffalo one day after football practice. I shared how I believed that when someone is filled with the Holy Spirit, he will speak in tongues as the evidence that he has been filled. I shared my belief based on scripture and not just my experience. However, my experience backed up what I had learned in the Book of Acts and other places in the Bible.

When I finished giving my beliefs and convictions on the Holy Spirit, a man sitting at the table, (who was the President of a major Christian organization, a very close friend of mine, and probably the most influential leader at this retreat), asked me the following question, "Mike do you believe that because you speak in tongues you have more of God than I do?"

Every eye was on me and the question was very out of character for this man, as he is the kind of person who accepts everyone. My testimony had been cut short. He was asking a question that could cause a divide in the close relationship that we all shared at that table. It obviously could affect us working together to reach teenagers across America as well.

I knew this question was a set-up because if I said no, I would be denying the importance of the Baptism with the Holy Spirit, and if I said yes, I would come across as spiritually arrogant. I was in a tough spot and I knew this was a defining moment in our meetings. As I was unsure of how I would answer, I said a silent prayer in my heart and asked the Lord if He would give me the wisdom to answer my brother's question.

Then I believe the Lord spoke to my heart and gave me the wisdom I needed. With every eye looking at me, I said the following words, "Brother, I don't believe that is the right question. The question is not, 'Do I think I have more of God than you do,' but the question is, 'Do you think you have all of God that is available to you?'"

The man looked at me and smiled and said, "That's a good answer." I didn't say it then, but in my heart I knew the Lord had given me a Word of Wisdom. I knew that it was not my answer, but it came from Jesus Himself.

Speaking in Tongues in Your Personal Prayer Life and Speaking in Tongues in the Church

I believe that every child of God, when he is baptized with the Holy Spirit, or filled with the Spirit, will receive the ability to speak with other tongues (which is also a Pentecostal Doctrine). This is a supernatural phenomenon whereby the recipient will have the ability to speak in a language that he has never learned. It has been called his "prayer language."

The Bible says that when we speak in tongues we don't speak unto man, but unto God and the benefit is for us personally: *"For he that speaketh in an unknown tongue speaketh not unto men, but unto God: for no man understandeth him; howbeit in the spirit he speaketh mysteries"* (I Cor. 14:2).

The Apostle Paul describes the special usage of this prayer language in I Cor. 14:14-15 when he says, *"If I pray in an unknown tongue, my spirit prayeth, but my understanding is unfruitful. What is it then? I will pray with the spirit, and I will pray with the understanding also: I will sing with the spirit, and I will sing with the understanding also."*

So there is a distinct advantage that a believer has when he can pray and sing in the spirit as well as in understanding. Both are important to the believer's prayer life. However, when one speaks in tongues in a church service, it is an entirely different use of this gift. Praying in tongues is for the believer's personal prayer life and speaking in tongues in the Church is for the edification of others.

Notice Paul says, *"I thank my God, I speak with tongues more than ye all: Yet in the Church I had rather speak five words with my understanding, that by my voice I might teach others also, than ten thousand words in an unknown tongue"* (I Cor. 14:18-19).

Many of the eager and zealous Christians in the early Church who had been filled with the Holy Spirit were using their spiritual gift of Tongues publicly and it was causing confusion in the Church at Corinth. Paul was teaching them how to use the gifts properly and in order for the edification of all.

Paul taught that if the gift of Tongues was going to be used publicly in the service it needed to be interpreted in the language that all knew so they could understand what was being said. He gave clear instructions:

"If any man speak in an unknown tongue, let it be by two or at the most by three, and that by course; and let one in-

terpret. But if there be no interpreter, let him keep silence in the church; and let him speak to himself, and to God" (I Cor. 14:27-28).

Paul gave pretty clear instructions to the Church at Corinth. He limited the use of tongues in public service to two or three people giving a word of encouragement. These messages were to be interpreted, and if no interpreter was present then this gift was not to be used.

These instructions seem pretty clear and orderly with no room for confusion, right? Well the problem is we have many churches today that don't follow Paul's instructions. It should be remembered that these are not Paul's words, but God's Words and we are to follow them if we want the Lord's blessing.

I have been in many Pentecostal and Charismatic churches that allow their congregants to speak in tongues openly in the meeting without interpretation. This has caused many in the Body of Christ to become confused. They will then use this to dismiss the gifts of the Spirit as confusing, thus causing division in the Body of Christ.

Paul said, *"If therefore the whole church be come together into one place, and all speak with tongues, and there come in those who are unlearned, or unbelievers, will they not say that ye are mad?"* (I Cor. 14:23).

If we would only follow the Word of God, we would find that the speaking with other Tongues is not confusing. It is a beautiful, powerful gift and a great witness to the unbeliever when it is used correctly. As Paul also said, *"But if all prophecy* (that includes tongues when it is followed by interpretation), *and there come in one that believeth not, or one unlearned, he is convinced of all, he is judged of all: And thus are the secrets of his heart made manifest; and so falling down on his face he will worship God, and report that God is in you of a truth"* (I Cor. 14:24-25).

So we see that there is a right way to conduct a service where the gifts of the Spirit are manifested and there is a wrong way to conduct a service where the gifts are manifested. Unfortunately, the wrong usage has caused many to not want anything to do with the gifts of the Spirit. They leave churches that preach and teach the gifts are for today, and they find churches that don't believe in, or practice, the gifts. You see how much damage we can do when we don't follow the Word as it is written? Much of the confusion today regarding the gifts of the Spirit can be traced to churches that have operated in the gifts incorrectly. In their zeal, many have unfortunately caused more damage than good.

We must hear the words of the Apostle Paul and follow them, *"Let all things be done decently and in order"* (I Cor. 14:40), *"For God is not the author of confusion"* (I Cor. 14:33). Let the church that operates in the gifts of the Spirit hear the Word of the Lord, *"But if there be no interpreter, let him keep silence in the church"* (I Cor. 14:28). This, by the way, is speaking of a church service and is not to limit the use of tongues among believers, but is simply speaking of order in the context of a service.

Do All Speak in Tongues?

The statement found in I Corinthians 12:30, *"Do all speak in other tongues?"* has been misunderstood and taught that speaking in other tongues is not for all believers. Therefore, it is suggested that since God wants every believer to be filled with the Holy Spirit (Eph. 5:18), tongues can't be the evidence that one has received the infilling of the Spirit.

First of all, one must look at the context in which Paul made this statement to the Corinthian Church. He is speaking about the gifts of the Spirit and the Body of Christ and how God functions differently within His Body. He said in I Cor. 12:28 (two verses earlier), *"And God has set some in the church..."* Paul is speaking here of the ministry that goes on in the church; he is not speaking of our personal relationship with Christ. The context in which he makes this statement *"do all speak with tongues,"* is in the context of the Body of Christ functioning in unison.

In the Expositor's New Testament, the explanation of I Cor. 12:30 is as follows: "Paul is not addressing himself here to the initial Baptism with the Spirit, which is always and without exception accompanied by speaking with other tongues, but rather is addressing the gift of Tongues, which all do not have, although Baptized with the Spirit."[2]

If Paul was speaking of tongues in general and saying that not all who are baptized with the Holy Spirit will speak with other tongues, then he would be contradicting what Jesus taught in Mark 16:17 when He said the sign of speaking with other tongues would follow them that believe. If one teaches that not all who are baptized with the Holy Spirit will speak in tongues, then Jesus' statement in Mark 16:17 is not correct. We know that this cannot be true. The teacher of that doctrine, whoever he may be, has a problem with the understanding of what the scripture is teaching. Satan has lied to him and convinced him to teach that tongues is not the initial evidence that one has been filled. Because this lie is believed and taught, we have a lot of people walking around saying, "I am filled with the Holy Spirit but I don't speak in tongues." The truth is that they have not been filled but they have been led to believe in a counterfeit baptism which is most tragic, as I am sure you can see.

So, there is the speaking with other tongues as your personal prayer language which one receives at the moment he is Baptized with the Holy Spirit, and then there is the gift of Tongues used in the Church when the Holy Spirit comes over a person to bring a word from God to His people, which always is to be accompanied with interpretation. The gift of Tongues is the same as speaking in other tongues, but they are used in two different ways.

The speaking with other tongues is the evidence that one has received the Baptism with the Holy Spirit (Acts 2:4), and it is for everyone who is born again. It is a personal "prayer language," for the Bible says, *"they were all filled with the Holy Ghost and began to speak with other tongues"* (Acts 2:4). God could have cleared up this whole confusion (as obviously He knew it would occur), by saying that "they were all filled and some spoke in tongues." But that is not what the scriptures say. When one receives the Baptism with the Holy Spirit, he will speak in other tongues just as Jesus said (Mark 16:17).

Unbelief always wants to make exceptions. Those who don't believe that God still heals today, or believe that He is not healing like He did in the Bible, will say, "God doesn't want to heal today," or, "Divine healing is not in the atonement." Yet, the scriptures say that Jesus healed all who came to Him in faith believing and the scriptures command the Church to anoint with oil the one who is sick and, *"the prayer of faith shall save the sick"* (James 5:15). In fact, Jesus didn't tell His disciples to pray for the sick and hope they would be healed, but He said, *"heal the sick"* (Matt. 10:8).

Then why aren't more people being healed today in America and Canada? The Bible says that, *"And he could there do no mighty work, save that he laid his hands upon a few sick folks, and healed them"* (Mark 6:5). This is the town of Nazareth where Jesus grew up. The people of His town could not accept this little boy, who grew up among them as the son of a carpenter, now as the "healing Messiah." They lacked faith. Unbelief always limits what God wants to do (Hebrews 11:6).

The Book of Acts and I Corinthians 12-14

Many pastors and teachers confuse the Book of Acts with what Paul was writing to the Corinthian Church in chapters 12-14. They say that Paul was explaining Acts in I Corinthians chapters 12-14. No, the letter Paul was writing was addressing a new problem that had arisen in the Church of Corinth that we did not see happening in the Book of Acts: the misuse of the gifts of the Spirit.

In the Book of Acts there are three instances where the speaking with other tongues is used:

"And they were all filled with the Holy Ghost, and began to speak with other tongues, as the Spirit gave them utterance." (Acts 2:4)

"For they heard them speak with tongues, and magnify God." (Acts 10:46)

"And when Paul had laid his hands upon them, the Holy Ghost came on them; and they spake with tongues, and prophesied" (Acts 19:6)

Notice in every instance that the scriptures in the book of Acts state that the "speaking with other tongues" was in the context of people receiving the Baptism with the Holy Spirit.

Now in the Book of I Corinthians (chapters 12-14), the speaking with other tongues is always used in the context of a church service. So, in this context, the usage of Tongues will be accompanied with the Interpretation of Tongues.

In I Corinthians 12:10 Paul writes, *"To another the working of miracles; to another prophecy; to another discerning of spirits, to another divers kinds of tongues; to another the interpretation of tongues."*

As you see, Paul, in referring to the gift of Tongues, speaks of interpretation with it. Why? Because he is speaking of the use of tongues in the church service. In understanding scripture, one must keep things in proper context. The whole context of I Corinthians 12 is speaking of the Body of Christ (I Cor. 12:13-14).

In I Cor. 12:30 Paul asked, *"Do all speak with tongues?"* He is asking this question in the context of the Church. Going back to this verse, we see in I Corinthians 11:18, *"For first of all, when ye come together in the church, I hear that there be divisions among you."* The context of chapters 11-14 is Paul giving instructions that are to clear up the divisions that were in the Corinthian Church. There were two main things causing the division in the Church:

1) The Lord's Supper was being taken incorrectly
2) The gifts of the Spirit were being used wrongly

Paul uses the word "church" 12 times in I Corinthian 11-14 and he uses the phrase "when ye come together" six times. So, the whole context of chapters 11-14 in the first letter to the Corinthian Church was to address the divisions that were being caused when they "came together."

Notice again, Paul, in addressing how the gifts of the Spirit are to be used, said, *"And God hath set some in the church"* (I Cor. 12:28). His analogy of the Church functioning correctly is the human body, and he says, *"If the whole body were an eye, where were the hearing? If the whole were hearing, where were the smelling?"* (I Cor. 12:17). Paul is addressing the problem of the disunity in the Church manifesting through the improper use of the gifts of the Spirit (i.e. the whole body wanting to speak in tongues in the service).

Why is this so important? It is important that you don't confuse the speaking with other tongues (i.e. personal prayer language) given to the individual at the Baptism with the Holy Spirit and the usage of the gift of Tongues in context of a church service. There are two distinct uses of the gift of speaking in Tongues, one for personal use and one for the edification of the Body (I Cor. 14:4, 12). The latter is always accompanied by the gift of Interpretation (I Cor. 14:5).

If you read the phrase *"do all speak with tongues?"* alone, or out of context, you could make a case that the speaking with other tongues is not a gift for every believer. However, now read in context and it will shed a different light, *"In the Church...do all speak with tongues?"* (I Cor. 12:28, 30).

When Paul says, *"have all the gifts of healing? do all speak with tongues? Do all interpret?"* these questions are all referring to the problem in the Corinthian Church with all the people exercising their spiritual gifts with no order. He tells them very specifically that if anyone speaks in tongues "in the church" it should be done with an interpreter present and it should only be done by two or, at the most, three. (I Cor. 14:27). So, Paul put a limit on the public usage of tongues in a public service and, again, there must be an interpreter present for it to be used at all.

Paul also said to the believers at Corinth, *"I thank my God, I speak with tongues more than ye all."* (I Cor. 14:18). So obviously, Paul was not saying tongues is only for a few choice servants, but it was for all, as he compared his thankfulness for tongues to the other believers. In other words, in this statement he is inferring that they all speak in tongues.

But, he said, *"Yet in the church I had rather speak five words with my understanding, that by my voice I might teach others also, than ten thousand words in an unknown tongue"* (I Cor. 14:19). So, the limits of tongues is not for individuals in their personal experience with God (i.e. the Baptism with the Holy Spirit), but in their manifesting that gift in the church.

Paul concludes this admonishment with the words, *"Wherefore, brethren, covet to prophesy, and forbid not to speak with tongues"* (I Cor. 14:39). He is not trying to minimize the importance of speaking with other tongues, but just trying to bring the house of God into order (I Cor. 14:40).

Speaking in Other Tongues is the "Sign Gift"

The Bible tells us that tongues is a sign gift to the world that Jesus is coming soon. Joel, the Holy Ghost prophet of the Old Testament, said, *"And it shall come to pass afterward, that I will pour out my spirit upon all flesh; and your sons and your daughters shall prophesy, your old men shall dream dreams, your young men shall see visions: And also upon the servants and upon the handmaids in those days will I pour out my spirit"* (Joel 2:28-29).

On the Day of Pentecost, Peter stood among the people and he quoted this verse (Acts 2:16-18) as to say, this which you see (the disciples filled with the Spirit and speaking with other tongues), is what the prophet forecasted would happen in the last days. Peter said, *"this is that,"* (Acts 2:16).

Every time you hear someone speaking in tongues, or when someone is baptized with the Holy Spirit with the evidence of speaking with other tongues, it is sending a message to the world: *"this is that,"* meaning we are living in the last days. Joel 2:30-31 says, *"And I will shew wonders in the heavens in the earth, blood, and fire, and pillars of smoke. The sun shall be turned into darkness, and the moon into blood, before the great and terrible day of the LORD come."*

The controversy over speaking in tongues is due to the devil trying to stop the demonstration of the power of the Spirit. He is intimidated by the "dunamis," the miraculous power of God. He knows that if the power of the Holy Spirit is allowed to move, his kingdom of darkness will be reduced greatly. So he fights to confuse and to divide the Church. Looking at the last 100 years in America, I have to admit the devil has been able to greatly deceive the Body of Christ.

The Body of Christ must come back to the scriptures and study the early Church in the book of Acts to realize that the power of the early Church was the Holy Ghost, and the power for the modern Church is the Holy Ghost. If we will not add to, or take away from, the Word of God, but simply believe all of it for today, then the confusion and the division would be eliminated. I believe we would see the kind of results the early Church saw.

> *"And they, continuing daily with one accord in the temple, and breaking bread from house to house, did eat their meat with gladness and singleness of heart, Praising God, and having favor with all the people. And the Lord added to the church daily such as should be saved."* (Acts 2:46-7)

Is Tongues for Today?

When Peter got up on the Day of Pentecost to explain to the people what was occurring in Jerusalem, as the Bible says, the people were amazed and marveled and said to one another *"Behold, are not all these which speak Galileans? And how hear we every man in our own tongue, wherein we were born?"* (Acts 2:7,8). Peter's explanation can be found in the first sermon ever preached in the New Testament Church in Acts 2:14-41.

As a result of this first sermon, the Bible tells us that 3,000 souls were saved. In Peter's sermon, he says something as if he knew that one day there would be preachers who would try to say that the Baptism of the Holy Spirit, evidenced by speaking in other tongues, would not be for their day. Obviously, it was the Holy Spirit who inspired Peter to preach these words to make sure that the Church would never try to say this gift has ceased. Take a close look at these important words of Peter regarding the Baptism with the Holy Spirit:

> *"For the Promise* (the Baptism with the Holy Spirit with the evidence of speaking with other tongues, Acts 1:4-5) *is unto you* (the Jews of that day), *and to your children* (means the great outpouring did not stop on the Day of Pentecost), *and to all who are afar off* (meaning

the whole world), *even as many as the Lord our God shall call."* (Acts 2:39)

That last statement of Peter in verse 39 *"even as many as the Lord our God shall call"* says it all. This verse tells us that every child of God who will ever be saved before Jesus comes again can receive the gift of the baptism with the Holy Spirit just like the 120 did in the Temple on the Day of Pentecost. Now ask the question based on Acts 2:39, why has the Body of Christ believed the lie that the gifts of the Holy Spirit are not for today or that God has changed how we receive the gift of Baptism with the Holy Spirit today?

If you have been taught this, you have been cheated out of the fullness of the greatest gift the Church has ever been given. Remember, 50 days before the Day of Pentecost, Peter would not stand up for Christ. He was afraid and tried to save his own skin. He denied knowing Christ. The Bible says that a certain maid beheld Peter as he sat by a fire warming himself on the night Jesus was betrayed, and the woman looked at Peter and said, *"'This man was also with him.' And he denied him, saying, 'Woman, I know him not'"* (Luke 22:56-57).

But, on the Day of Pentecost, after Peter was filled with the Holy Spirit (Acts 2:4), a boldness came on him that caused Peter to get up in front of thousands of people, risk persecution, imprisonment, even death, and preach the salvation message to the people of Jerusalem. The Bible says, *"But Peter, standing up with the eleven, lifted up his voice"* (Acts 2:14). What happened to make Peter so strong and courageous? He was baptized with the Holy Spirit with the evidence of speaking with other tongues.

So, you see, if the devil can convince the Church that the promise of the Holy Ghost is not for today, then he has caused the Church to be weakened and the boldness of the Spirit will be removed, not to mention the miraculous power of God. What could be more tragic than this?

Peter wouldn't stand up on the night before Christ was crucified because his flesh was fearful, but after he was filled with the Spirit, he stood up boldly. For the Body of Christ that has bought the lie that the Baptism with the Holy Ghost with the evidence of speaking with other tongues is not for today, it's time to repent of that teaching and believe that the Bible's message has not changed.

When you believe that the same power and the same demonstration of the early Church is for the modern Church, then, like Peter, you will be changed from operating in the flesh and you will become bold in the Spirit and you will "stand up!" The Church must realize the Baptism with the Holy Spirit with the evidence of speaking with other tongues does not belong to the Pentecostals or the Charismatics, but it belongs to the whole Body of Christ.

Chapter 12

HOW TO RECEIVE THE BAPTISM WITH THE HOLY SPIRIT

The Baptism with the Holy Spirit is for every child of God. It is not for a particular group of believers or a particular denomination. a, t stated in the previous chapter, the Baptism with the Holy Spirit does not belong to the Pentecostal denomination or Charismatic movement; it belongs to the Body of Christ.

When John the Baptist came on the scene, the Bible records some very important words that he said, *"I indeed baptize you with water unto repentance: but he that cometh after me is mightier than I, whose shoes I am not worthy to bear: he shall baptize you with the Holy Ghost, and with fire"* (Matt.3:11).

The very purpose for the coming of the Messiah was to redeem man from sin and to baptize believers with the Holy Spirit. His mission was to forgive and remove sin so that the Holy Spirit could take up residence in the believer's heart, thereby restoring each sinner into right relationship with God. It is the Holy Spirit who does the work of conversion made possible through the Cross of Christ.

The Baptism with the Holy Spirit is to give the believer in Christ a deeper power to witness and to be a witness in his actions (Acts 1:8). The fire of the Holy Spirit comes with conviction to burn out the sins of our flesh so that the world will see a change in us. Matthew says, *"Whose fan is in his hand to thoroughly purge his floor, and gather his wheat into the garner; but he will burn up the chaff with unquenchable fire"* (Matt. 3:12).

How Does One Receive This Baptism?

To answer this question you must go to the places in the Bible where the Holy Spirit was poured out and believers received. The beginning was on the Day of Pentecost and the Bible says that they tarried ten days before the promise of the Father came, which is the Baptism with the Holy Spirit (Acts 1:4-5, 2:1). Some have taught that you have to "tarry" or "wait" for the Baptism with the Holy Spirit, but that was specifically true of those who waited in the upper room for the Holy Spirit. Now that the Day of Pentecost has fully come (Acts 2:1), we no longer have to wait for a specific number of days. However, there are certain conditions which must be met.

What are the Conditions for Receiving?

First, the person asking to be baptized with the Holy Spirit must be saved. The Lord will not give the gift of the Holy Spirit to an unbeliever. Jesus said, *"And I will pray the Father, and he shall give you another Comforter, that he may abide with you for ever; Even the Spirit of truth; whom the world cannot receive, because it seeth him not, neither knoweth him: but you know him; for he dwelleth with you, and shall be in you"* (John14:16,17).

The believers in Acts 2, who received the Baptism with the Holy Spirit, were already saved. The 70 were given authority and sent out by Jesus to minister. When they returned, they shared with Jesus their amazement that even the demons were subject to them through His Name. Jesus said to them, *"Notwithstanding in this rejoice not, that the spirits are subject unto you; but rather rejoice, because your names are written in heaven"* (Luke 10:20).

In the very next chapter we see recorded that Jesus was teaching on prayer and He said these words, *"If ye then, being evil, know how to give good gifts unto your children: how much more shall your heavenly Father give the Holy Ghost to those who ask him?"* (Luke 11:13)

So, we see that the gift of the Holy Spirit (i.e. the Baptism with the Holy Spirit) is only given to God's children. Why is this? Because the work of redemption, Christ's cleansing from all sin, makes way for the Holy Spirit to take up residency in the believer's heart. Now, the work of Christ, when believed by the confessing sinner, "purges the floor" so that the Holy Spirit can fill the believer.

Secondly, notice by the above verse, Luke 11:13, that we must ask for the gift of the Holy Spirit. The Baptism with the Holy Spirit, just like salvation, is not automatic. We must ask our Father in heaven. As James tells us (James 4:2), *"yet you have not, because you ask not."*

Many in the Body of Christ have never asked to be filled with the Holy Spirit. Perhaps this is due to a lack of knowledge. When Paul came upon the disciples of John in Ephesus, he asked them the question, *"Have ye received the Holy Ghost since ye believed?"* (Acts 19:2). Now if the Baptism with the Holy Spirit was automatic at salvation (as some teach), there would be no reason for Paul to ask that question.

The disciples responded to Paul's question by saying, *"We have not so much as heard whether there be any Holy Ghost."* They had not received the Baptism with the Holy Spirit because they had not asked, and they had not asked because they did not know that the Holy Spirit had come.

God, speaking through the prophet Hosea, said these words, *"My people are destroyed for lack of knowledge"* (Hosea 4:6). Many believers have not asked to be filled with the Spirit because they do not know or have not heard that there is a subsequent encounter with the Holy Spirit after salvation.

The Bible says, *"For by grace are ye saved through faith"* (Eph. 2:8). Everything that God gives us is by grace, meaning we don't deserve it and we can't work for it. We can only receive by faith, meaning we believe that what Christ did on the Cross makes it possible.

When I personally received the Baptism with the Holy Spirit, I was praying and asking God to fill me. As I was praying with another believer, who was agreeing for me to receive the gift of Tongues, I became somewhat frustrated. My friend who was praying for me was speaking in another tongue, but I was speaking in English. I did not know what to do or how to receive. My friend said, "Mike, start speaking the words I am saying." After attempting that for a few seconds, I felt very foolish as it was just gibberish and didn't sound anything like my friend's tongue.

But then, in my misunderstanding, I did something vitally important. I asked God. I remember asking the Lord, "How do I receive the gift of Tongues?" The Lord spoke to my heart very clearly and I will never forget it. He said, "How did you receive your salvation?" To which I responded, "By faith," and the Lord said to me, "So receive the gift of Tongues."

I went back to attempting to speak in tongues, but this time it was different. I didn't try to mimic my friend's tongue. I spoke in gibberish out loud and I had faith that, at any second, He was going to give me my new language. It was only a few seconds before this glorious language began to come out of my mouth.

The sounds coming from my mouth were truly miraculous. Although I could not understand the words, as they were unknown to me, nonetheless, I could sense the power of the Holy Spirit. It was a "sign" and it was a "wonder." A sign that I had been filled with Holy Spirit just like the believers in the Book of Acts and it was a wonder of the dunamis, the miraculous power of the Holy Spirit. Wow, what a moment in my spiritual journey, one that I have never quite gotten over. The benefits that have come with that new beginning have been nothing short of glorious in my life and are for every believer in Christ who will ask in faith.

There must be a hunger and thirst in the child of God for all that the Lord wants to give him. The believer may have the sense that there is something missing in his relationship with God. Jesus taught, in the Sermon on the Mount, *"Blessed are they which do hunger and thirst after righteousness* (this means intense desire): *for they shall be filled"* (Matt. 5:6).

Lastly, but by no means least, you must surrender all to the Lord. You must yield your members unto God. What are your members? They are your eyes, your hands, your feet, your tongue, any part that causes you to sin. Yield your members to Him to be used for righteousness. What does it mean to yield? It means to let Him lead. *"Neither yield ye your members as instruments of unrighteousness, unto sin: but yield yourselves unto God, as those that are alive from the dead, and your members as instruments of righteousness unto God"* (Romans 6:13).

Many times there is a lack of repentance in a certain area in the life of the believer, and it blocks the ability of God to fill them. Just as repentance is a condition for receiving the indwelling of the Holy Spirit at salvation (Mark 1:15), it is also needed at the moment of being baptized with the Holy Spirit. Unconfessed sin or unforgiveness is always a hindrance to receiving from God. *"Behold, the LORD's hand is not shortened, that it cannot save; neither his ear heavy, that it cannot hear: But your iniquities have separated between you and your God, and your sins have hid his face from you, that he will not hear"* (Isa.59:1,2).

I think there is a reason why the Baptism of Water (which represents repentance) is so closely associated with the Baptism with the Holy Spirit. The two go together. When Jesus was baptized by John in the Jordan River, immediately upon coming up out of the waters the scripture says that the heavens were opened and the Spirit of God was seen descending like a dove (a symbol of the Holy Spirit) upon Him. Obviously Jesus never sinned and didn't need to repent, but He was baptized as the model of what we are to do. From this, we can see the close association between repentance and Spirit Baptism. There is more evidence in scripture of this close association (Matt. 3:11, Acts 2:38,39, 8:12-15, 9:17,18, 10;44-48, 19:1-6).

Check your heart's motive for asking for the Baptism with the Holy Spirit; is it pure? Do you want the Baptism with the Holy Spirit for no other reason than to be closer to Jesus and to be more effective in reaching a lost world for Him? The Bible says that people ask God for things but don't receive them because they *"ask amiss, that ye may consume it upon your lusts"* (James 4:3). This word "amiss" means "to ask improperly." If you want this gift for your own personal use so you can say, "I have the gift of Tongues," then don't expect to receive. The Lord can read your heart.

So, if your heart is pure and repentant, if your spirit is thirsty for all of Him, and you have the faith to believe, ask God right now to baptize you with His Holy Spirit, and to give you the evidence of speaking with other tongues. Let's pray! (This is a suggested prayer for you to put in your own words and mean it with your whole heart.)

Dear Heavenly Father, I come to You in Jesus' Name. I am hungry and thirsty for more of You. I want to be filled with Your Holy Spirit and I believe that Jesus Christ is the baptizer. I repent right now and turn from every sin that stands in the way of receiving all that You have for me. I surrender every member of my being to be used for

Your glory without reservation. I want all that You have planned for my life, every gift that You choose to give me to minister to others in Your Name. Use me, empower me, and equip me for Your kingdom work. I ask now for the Baptism of the Holy Spirit with the evidence of speaking with other tongues.

In Jesus' Name I pray, Amen.

After saying this prayer, I would encourage you to begin to move your tongue and begin to speak words that are not your natural language by faith. The words may begin to come out of your mouth in gibberish, but I believe as you begin to move your tongue by faith, believing that any minute God is going to give you the ability to speak in an unknown language, that He will do it. Begin right now!

I trust that God has gloriously baptized you with His Holy Spirit with the evidence of speaking with other tongues, and I rejoice with you at this amazing moment in your spiritual walk with Him.

I want to encourage you, if you did not receive the gift of the Holy Spirit at this present moment, continue to ask, seek and knock. I know the testimonies of many people who would not give up and God did give them exactly what they asked for in due time. In fact, a friend of mine told me that she locked herself in her bedroom and told God, "I am not coming out until you baptize me with your Holy Spirit." I asked this person how long she was in there, and she said eight hours. But she said, "After eight hours I came out of that room speaking in other tongues as the Spirit gave me the utterance." Glory to God! True faith will not stop asking

"And I say unto you, Ask, and it shall be given you; seek and ye shall find; knock, and it shall be opened unto you. For every one that asketh receiveth; and he that seeketh findeth; and to him that knocketh it shall be opened.

If a son shall ask bread of any of you that is a father, will he give him a stone? Or if he ask a fish, will he for a fish give him a serpent? Or if he shall ask an egg, will he offer him a scorpion? If ye then, being evil, know how to give good gifts unto your children: how much more shall your heavenly Father give the Holy Spirit to them that ask him?" (Luke 11:9-13).

When the Lord baptizes you with His Holy Spirit and you receive the evidence of speaking with other tongues would you be so kind to give a witness and email me, announcing that you have received? I wrote this book for you, and the only thing I asked from the Lord in return was that He would use this book as an inspiration for many to ask for the Mighty River to fill them and that many would be gloriously filled. You can email me at mikec@joshuarevolution.org.

Chapter 13

THE AZUSA STREET REVIVAL

In writing this book on the Holy Spirit, I felt it was very important to look at some historical moves of God where the Holy Spirit's power had been poured out. There is much we can learn in revival, and the revival that has always intrigued me the most has been the Azusa Street Revival.

In the spring of 2006, I traveled to the City of Angels, Los Angeles, California for the 100 year Centennial of the Azusa Street Revival. Historians called this the most powerful revival since the Day of Pentecost. I went to that conference wanting to learn why God chose that place and that group of people on which to pour out His Spirit so greatly.

As I sought the Lord during my time in Los Angeles, my constant plea to God was, "Please show me what it was that caused you to move so greatly 100 years ago at the Azusa Mission." I sensed the Lord respond to my plea by saying, "I want you to learn everything you can about William Seymour."

William J. Seymour was born in 1870. He is known as the Pastor of the great Azusa Street Revival. This move of God started on April 9, 1906 and lasted until October of 1909. For three and a half years, this revival shook America and the world. The aftershocks are still being felt today and Brother Seymour has become one of the most influential and respected Pentecostal leaders of all time.

Brother Seymour was an African American man who was blind in one eye and walked with a limp. His father and mother were slaves and he grew up in a very poor family. He would receive his Bible education at a school where segregation laws prevented him from sitting in the classroom with the other white students, so he would sit in the hallway and listen with his ear pushed up against the door.

It was said about Seymour that he was one of the meekest men you would ever meet. His prayer life was dynamic as he would pray, on average, 5-6 hours a day. He had a passion to witness a move of the Holy Spirit in his day. He prayed for this constantly. He knew there was more to God than what he was experiencing. He desired to be filled with the Holy Spirit and to see the supernatural power be demonstrated as it was in the early Church. He was a man that would not just settle for mediocre Christianity, but he wanted to see biblical Christianity in his day. He wanted to see another Book of Acts Church.

William Seymour was reared in a Catholic home just a few miles from the Gulf Coast in southern Louisiana. He enrolled in the Charles Parham Bible School in Houston, Texas in January 1906. Charles Parham was the man who introduced Brother Seymour to the Baptism with the Holy Spirit. In fact, there were five cardinal teachings Charles Parham taught that Brother Seymour accepted and later taught. These five doctrinal truths served as the foundation of the Azusa Street Mission's teaching. They were:

1) Justification by Faith

2) Sanctification as a definite work of grace

3) Baptism with the Holy Spirit evidenced by speaking in other tongues

4) Divine Healing is in the Atonement of Christ

5) The personal premillennial rapture of the saints at the second coming of Christ

These five doctrines preached and taught by Brother Seymour also became the foundation to Pentecostalism which followed the Azusa movement. They taught that Jesus is Savior, Sanctifier, Spirit Baptizer, Healer, and Coming King!

Author Grant McClung wrote in his book *Azusa Street: 100 years of Commentary*, "Pentecostalism has been strongly influenced by the premillennial/dispensational view of the second coming of Christ. Reference to the imminence of Christ's return punctuated the revival's rhetoric and fueled enthusiasm for evangelism. Early Pentecostals were certain they were living in the end-time restoration of New Testament apostolic power. For example, Seymour declared that the Azusa Street revival is 'the' last revival before the coming of the Lord, and that, for them, all earthly history would soon be consummated by the 'Rapture." The early Pentecostals reasoned that signs and wonders were powerful indications of Christ's imminent return. Little wonder, then, that they evangelized with such explosive dynamism. Many even departed immediately, without adequate financing or missionary training, to far-flung destinations. This strong conviction of Christ's soon coming again impacted Pentecostal missionary practice. In fact, it is still proceeding from an inherent 'last day mission theology.' And throughout Pentecostal literature, yet today, one finds references to a 'last-day ministry', or that 'time is growing short,' or that the second coming of Christ will 'be very, very soon.'[1]

The Azusa Street teaching centered on the Baptism with the Holy Spirit, with the evidence of speaking with other tongues. Brother Seymour, although he had not yet personally received the Baptism with the Holy Spirit, still taught it. He strongly believed that the gift of Tongues was the evidence that one had been baptized with the Holy Spirit. It became one of the early Pentecostal distinctives.

Shortly after enrolling in Charles Parham's Bible school, Seymour received an invitation to go to Los Angeles and preach at a black holiness church. He traveled by train and when he arrived for the meetings, Brother Seymour, on the second night of the meetings, preached on the Baptism with the Holy Spirit with the "initial evidence" of speaking with other tongues. Brother Seymour preached that one cannot claim to be Baptized with the Holy Spirit if they did not have the evidence of speaking with other tongues as the church had done on the day of Pentecost (Acts 2:1-4). This was revolutionary teaching and it was offensive to that congregation and the Pastor rejected the teaching of Seymour.

When Brother Seymour returned the next night to preach, he found the church door locked and a sign on the door that read the meetings with William Seymour had been cancelled. Without money, not knowing what to do or where to go, Brother Seymour accepted an invitation from a couple in the church to stay at their home. His thought was just to return to the Bible School in Houston as soon as possible. However God had others plans for him, to say the least.

214 Bonnie Brea

As Seymour prayed each night with this couple in the parlor of their home, God began to move powerfully. They asked him if they could invite some of their friends to come over for Bible study and prayer. The prayer meeting soon grew too large for their tiny home, and they moved it to the home of Richard and Ruth Asbery at 214 Bonnie Brea in Los Angeles. This home today is the memorial site known as the place where the Azusa Street Revival actually began.

At Bonnie Brea on April 9, 1906, the Bible study was visited by the Holy Spirit. A woman by the name of Jenny Moore (who would later be married to William Seymour) received the Baptism with the Holy Spirit and went over to the piano. Although she had never taken a lesson, she sat down, and began to play beautifully and sing in tongues.

Soon, others were receiving the Baptism with the Holy Spirit with the evidence of speaking with other tongues. The Holy Spirit was moving so strongly in these meetings at 214 Bonnie Brea that it became a front porch meeting. They even filled the street in front of the house to listen to Brother Seymour preach and pray. One night the weight of the people caused the front porch to collapse and, although no one was hurt, they knew it was time to find a bigger location. They rented an old, vacant horse stable at 312 Azusa and it soon became known as the Azusa Mission.

At the Mission, God continued to move in a powerful way pouring out His Holy Spirit. Many said they had received the infilling and were speaking in other tongues. The media caught wind of these meetings and the Los Angeles Times, on April 18, 1906, called tongues a "weird babel" and called Seymour's followers a "sect of fanatics." However, the negative press just added to more numbers of people coming to check out what was going on at 312 Azusa. The devil always overplays his hand.[2]

It's a Revival!

As time passed, Brother Seymour and the people at Azusa claimed that all the gifts of the Spirit had been restored to the Church. Many people were being saved, miraculously healed, filled with the Spirit and revived to the call of the Great Commission. People from all over the world were traveling to Los Angeles to take part in the meetings.

From April 1906 to October 1909, they held three meetings a day. Sometimes one meeting just flowed into another. At other times they lasted into the wee hours of the night. Although tongue speaking was the center of attention, healing wasn't far behind. Historians reported that the walls inside of the Mission were lined with crutches, canes, and wheelchairs of people who had been healed.

In my search to find "clues" of why God moved so powerfully at Azusa Street, I found some amazing keys as to why I believe God chose the Azusa Mission as a place to pour out His Spirit in a way that has literally touched the world like no other revival since Pentecost.

First, it was the man, William Seymour. He was a man of prayer. It was said that he would put his head in an apple crate during the prayer meetings and he would sometimes keep his head in there for hours before he would minister. Brother Seymour was a man of prayer who would not do anything until he first heard from God about what He wanted him to do.

The prayer life of Jesus models this for us. Before Jesus did anything, He first went to His Father in prayer. Notice the day before the Lord chose His twelve disciples, the Bible says, *"And it came to pass in those days, that he went out into a mountain to pray, and continued all night in prayer to God. And when it was day, he called unto him his disciples: and of them he chose twelve, whom also he named apostles"* (Luke 6:12-13).

Brother Seymour also believed we are not to change the Bible. What the Bible taught and emphasized is what the Church should teach and emphasize. One of his favorite verses, that he wrote in almost all of his writings, was Jude 1:3 which says, *"Beloved, when I gave all diligence to write unto you of the common salvation, it was needful for me to write unto you, and exhort you that ye should earnestly contend for the faith which was once delivered unto the saints."*

Brother Seymour was not a man to compromise doctrine for the sake of unity. He preached and taught the Word of God with vigor and conviction. To *"earnestly contend for the faith"* in the Greek means "to struggle or fight for."[3]

Many churches today are teaching that we should just accept everyone and be tolerant in our differences and don't separate over doctrine. The so-called "faith preachers" today want to tell you to just be positive, and don't say anything negative. However, I will remind you that the prophets of old would declare before the people, "thus saith the Lord." They were not man-pleasers but they delivered the message of God to the people.

Much of the Apostle Paul's writings were warnings against certain doctrinal errors and calls to stand up against them. He said, *"If any man preach any other gospel unto you than that ye have received, let him be accursed"* (Galatians 1:9). This word "accursed" means "to be excommunicated." Paul, in his letter to Titus, wrote about how to deal with false teachers, *"A man that is an heretic* (false teacher), *after the first and second admonition, reject"* (Titus 3:10). If a false teacher is confronted about his error in his teaching and he doesn't repent of it, you are to go to him a second time and if he still keeps teaching it, you are to totally reject that teacher, no matter who he is. This is strong but it is right, obviously, because it is the Word of God. When you consider the fact that we are dealing with eternal life and the place where people will go after they die, one understands that there is no room for error.

Everyone knew what William Seymour stood for and he was not going to water that down for the sake of unity. God poured out His Spirit on Azusa because they preached and taught the main doctrines of the faith.

A.S. Worrell, translator of the New Testament, declared the "Azusa" work had rediscovered the blood of Christ to the

Church at that time. Great emphasis was placed on the "blood," for cleansing, etc.[4]

Wherever the Cross of Christ is preached and the power of the Holy Spirit is allowed to have His way, you are going to see God move in a powerful way. The modern Church is focused more on making the "seeker" comfortable than making the One whom we seek pleased with our worship.

God shows us through past revivals what He desires the Church to look like. We see in the Book of Acts what it was that moved the hand of God. I want to point out six things that I see precede a move of God and three things that follow a move of God.

Six Things that Precede a Move of God

1) A Dissatisfaction

There needs to be dissatisfaction with the way the Church is. When you look in the Book of Acts and you look at the Church today you see that, for the most part, they don't look the same. Before God moves in a great way, he finds a man who is not satisfied with the status quo and is desperate to see that change.

2) A Hatred for Sin

A conviction of sin must be present. The Church must hate sin and desire to be cleansed from all defilement of the world. The Bible says in Daniel 1:8, *"But Daniel purposed in his heart that he would not defile himself with the portion of the king's meat, nor with the wine which he drank:"* God moved greatly in the life of Daniel as a result of his heart not wanting to be defiled.

3) Repentance

There must be a cry to repent and the Church must respond. God sent John the Baptist to preach repentance before the coming of the Lord. John said: *"Repent ye: for the kingdom of heaven is at hand"* (Matthew 3:2). The word "repent" means to "turn around." The Church today, for the most part, is going in the wrong direction and it needs to turn around and go in the opposite direction.

4) Sound Doctrine

Proper doctrine must be preached and taught, the Cross of Christ being the emphasis, if you are to see a move of God. The Lord poured out His Spirit 50 days after Jesus died on the Cross. You will always see a close proximity between the Cross and the outpouring of the Holy Spirit.

5) Faith

Proper faith in Jesus Christ and Him crucified always pleases God. If our faith is in anything else, then the Spirit of God is grieved (saddened) and thereby quenched. The scriptures tell us *"But without faith it is impossible to please him"* (Heb. 11:6a). Proper faith is what pleases God. The Apostle Paul, the man to whom God gave the revelation of grace, said these words: *"For I determined not to know any thing among you, save Jesus Christ, and him crucified"* (I Cor. 2:2). This is the kind of faith that pleases God, and only this.

6) Prayer and Fasting

Prayer and fasting precede a move of God. In the Old Testament, the one day of the year that God required everyone to fast was on the Day of Atonement. However, men of God fasted much longer such as Moses, who fasted for 40 days. In the New Testament, Jesus fasted 40 days and 40 nights. When the Pharisees questioned Jesus as to why His disciples didn't fast, He said: *"Can the children of the bridechamber mourn, as long as the bridegroom is with them? But the days will come, when the bridegroom shall be taken from them, and then shall they fast"* (Matt.9:15).

The Bridegroom, Jesus Christ, has been taken so we are to fast now. As our youth pastor, Charlie, says, "When we fast, God moves fast." That is, if the fast is done with the right motive and understanding. But if the Church fasts and thinks God owes them something because they have fasted, then their heart is not in the right place and they can't properly understand fasting.

How is the Church supposed to look at fasting? First of all, you must understand fasting is not the answer to the believer's problem. To say that it is, means that you are circumventing the Cross. Jesus Christ is the answer to every problem of man. Placing one's faith in the finished work of Christ is the answer. I John 5:4 says, *"For whosoever is born of God overcometh the world: and this is the victory that overcometh the world, even our faith."*

Now we know that faith in the Cross of Christ is the answer. However, sometimes faith is eroded or slowed by the working of the flesh. So, the Christian needs to pray and fast to set aside the desires of the flesh (i.e. food) so faith can be in full operation.

In Mark chapter 9, a father brings his demon-stricken son to the disciples and asks them to heal him. They pray, but they cannot cast out the evil spirit from the boy. The father then takes him to Jesus and tells Jesus that the disciples could not cast out the spirit. Jesus says these words, *"O faithless generation, how long shall I be with you? how long shall I suffer you?"* (Mark 9:19). Jesus then goes on to heal the young boy. Sometime later, the disciples come to Jesus and ask Him why they could not cast out the spirit. Jesus says something very interesting. He says, *"This kind can come forth by nothing, but by prayer and fasting"* (Mark 9:29).

So, first of all we see that due to a lack of faith they could not cast out the spirit. Then we see Jesus telling His disciples that it was due to a lack of prayer and fasting as well.

Here is what I believe Jesus is revealing to His disciples and to us today. The answer to all problems is the blood of Christ and faith in the blood is what propels the Spirit to heal, deliver, save, etc. However, the flesh is the enemy of faith. When a Christian removes his own fleshly desires (i.e. eating), he then is more open to hear the Spirit of God; such is the need in the Church to fast and pray. Fasting and prayer are not the answers to sin. The answer is faith in what Jesus Christ did on the Cross, but prayer and fasting puts you into the place to appropriate faith in a greater way.

Think of it like an artery in the human body. The blood needs to travel through the artery to all parts of the body. If the blood is hindered in any way you have big problems. One of the main things that hinders the blood is cholesterol, a fatty substance that builds up over time on the inside of the artery walls. The cholesterol is like our flesh that hinders the blood of Christ from working. So, what you have to do is clean out the artery by removing the cholesterol (the flesh) so that the blood can flow freely.

The act of fasting is what God has given us to cleanse the body and to spiritually get us into a place where our faith is at another level to believe God for miracles. As they say, "new levels, new devils." If we want to go to another level with God and exercise authority over demon spirits, God has instructed us that it is achieved through prayer and fasting.

Three Things That Follow a Move of God

1) Miracles Happen

When God pours out His Spirit, miracles will follow. We see this on the Day of Pentecost. God poured out His Spirit on the 120 disciples who were praying, and probably fasting, and waiting on God. When the Spirit of God was poured out, we see men and women speaking in languages they had never learned before (Acts 2:4-11). This was a spiritual phenomenon, never seen by man before and on that same day 3,000 souls were saved. God's Spirit being poured out always results in miracles.

At Azusa Street, many sick bodies were healed as a result of God pouring out His Spirit. The blind saw, the lame walked, the deaf heard and God's deliverance was experienced by thousands.

2) The Great Commission is Emphasized

When the Holy Spirit was poured out at Azusa, people came from all over the world to visit and to experience firsthand this spiritual awakening. They were touched, moved, filled by the Holy Spirit, and boldness for world evangelism came upon them. They returned home with a new fervor to take the Gospel to the world. Many who lived in Los Angeles, or in other parts of America, came to visit the mission on Azusa Street and heard the call of God to be missionaries overseas and around the world.

One must realize that the Baptism of the Holy Spirit is the power of God to be a witness as Jesus had proclaimed it would be, *"But ye shall receive power, after that the Holy Ghost is come upon you: and ye shall be witnesses unto me both in Jerusalem, and in all Judaea, and in Samaria, and unto the uttermost part of the earth"* (Acts 1:8).

The Holy Spirit is always given to glorify Christ to a lost world! The Spirit is the One who gives us the fuel, the boldness and abandonment of our own personal lives to get the Gospel to the world. This is the essence of the mighty Baptism with the Holy Spirit. The call of God is to "become fishers of men" (Matt. 4:19), but how one does that is by the Baptism with the Holy Spirit.

3) Persecution

Every time there is a move of God, the religious spirits are going to be activated and persecution will immediately follow. We see this all through the Gospels and in the Book of Acts. When the lame man, who was sitting by the Temple gate, was healed by Peter and John, 5,000 souls came to Christ because of this one miracle. The religious leaders became very angry and hostile toward Peter and John. They tried to shut them up and stop the movement (Acts 4:1-22). Although they failed in their attempts, they still created many problems for the disciples.

One has to remember that revival is not accepted by all, particularly the religious. Why? Mainly due to jealously and envy which is the very sin that put Christ on the Cross. The religious leaders of Jesus' day hated Christ because He spoke against their traditions. He was the man that the people were following, which meant they were not following the religious leaders and this meant less money in the Temple treasury. This was the evil that was behind their hatred for Christ.

We Need Another Azusa!

If the Azusa Street Revival would be studied again, the Church would see that the Lord moved in a broken-down old building on a humble, hungry group of nobodies who were tired of old, dead religion and wanted more of God. These men and women were willing to repent and wait on God with prayer and fasting. It was there that God poured out His Spirit and touched the world through them. If the Church would again go this way, then maybe, just maybe, we would see God pour out His Spirit one more time.

In the Bible, the number seven is the number of completeness. We see that the Tribulation period is a seven-year period broken up into two three and a half year periods. The Azusa Street Revival lasted three and a half years. Could it be that God is going to pour out His Spirit one more time for three and a half years just prior to the Tribulation?

If you remember in Genesis 41, Joseph interpreted Pharaoh's dream and prophesied that there would be seven years of plenty and then seven years of famine. Pharaoh used this insight and during the seven years of plenty he built a storehouse and stored food and supplies. When the famine hit, he was ready and he made a lot of money as everyone came to him for their grain. The time of that famine is known as a type of the coming Tribulation, the last three and a half years of which is known as the Great Tribulation, or "Jacob's trouble," when all of Israel will be under attack (Jer. 30:7).

Now, if the seven years of famine were a type of the seven years of Tribulation that is just ahead, could it be that the seven years of plenty is a prophetic picture of seven years of harvest? Interesting enough is that, when the Spirit of God was being poured out at Azusa Street, the people believed that Jesus was coming very soon. But could it be that, for some reason, God stopped the revival at three and a half years and paused between the beginning of the revival and the end of the revival? In the Book of Revelation, God paused at the three and a half year mark after the seventh seal was broken, which was the last seal. The Bible says in Rev. 8:1, *"And when he had opened the seventh seal, there was silence in heaven about the space of half an hour."*

When one looks at the name "AZUSA" could there be a prophetic message in the name? The letter "A" is the first letter of the alphabet and "Z" is the last letter of the alphabet and the last three letters "USA." Could God be saying to us that Azusa was the Alpha Revival, the beginning of the last great revival in America before the Tribulation period, and there is another three and a half year revival coming to America: the "Z" or Omega Revival? Only God knows, but one thing is sure, we really need another Azusa Street Revival in America!

Chapter 14

THE RIVER OF GOD

In John 7:37-39, Jesus stood and cried out on the last day of the Feast of Tabernacles and said: *"If any man thirst, let him come unto me, and drink. He that believeth on me, as the scripture hath said, out of his belly shall flow rivers of living water. (But this spake he of the Spirit, which they who believe on him should receive: for the Holy Ghost was not yet given; because that Jesus was not yet glorified.)"*

This "River" of the Holy Spirit is not stationary, but it is moving, as the scripture says, *"shall flow rivers of living water."* From this, we know that Jesus is describing God the Holy Spirit as a vital, refreshing, and powerful moving, life-giving source for anyone who believes on Christ.

Water From The Rock

We see more symbolism of water as a type of the Holy Spirit in Exodus 17. Moses was leading the children of Israel in the wilderness and the people begin to complain because they were thirsty and there was no water. Only in the desert could God reveal Himself to the children of Israel. People in Israel have a saying that the wilderness is the place where "God speaks." It is the place to go to hear from God.

God waited until they became thirsty and cried out before He would provide the water. There is a great lesson here for all of us. God waits for His Church to become thirsty and willing to cry out for the Living Water before He sends the rain. God wants you to want Him.

Unfortunately, the lack of water caused the people's faith to waver, as they said to Moses, *"Wherefore is this that thou hast brought us up out of Egypt, to kill us and our children and our cattle with thirst?"* (Exodus 17:3).

They had just witnessed the parting of the Red Sea and saw how God rescued them from their enemies. However, their physical need blinded them from the previous miracles. Oh, how quickly man forgets the things that God has done to bring him to the point he is presently at. Friend, just remember, God hasn't brought you this far to leave you now.

Moses, witnessing the people's anger and not knowing what to do, went to the Lord. He interceded for God's wisdom and direction (Exodus 17:4). God instructed Moses to "go" before the people and take the rod that he had used to part the Red Sea in his hand (Exodus 17:5). We serve a "go forward" God. Two-thirds of God's name is "Go" and, unfortunately, too many in the Church are a stationary group of complainers.

God told Moses to strike the Rock in Horeb and from it would come forth an abundance of water for the people to drink (Exodus 17:6).

Moses obeyed the command of the Lord and, sure enough, when he struck the Rock, water gushed forth. Now, this is one of the most beautiful typologies found anywhere in Scripture. The Rock is Christ, the rod represents the Cross and the water symbolizes the Holy Spirit.

A Continuous Flow of the Spirit

Don't miss this amazing truth! It is the key to the victorious Christian life and the constant flow of the Holy Spirit. The water, typifying the Holy Spirit, is given to thirsty and desperate humanity through faith in the Cross (the rod) of Christ (the

Rock). This truth does not stop at the day of your conversion, but it is a truth that remains throughout your existence on this side of heaven. There is a Law of the Holy Spirit, that cannot be changed, that says the Mighty River (the Holy Spirit) is only supplied to man on a daily basis based upon his or her faith in Christ and Him crucified (Romans 8:2).

For the child of God to keep the River flowing, he must keep his faith in the Rock and, remember, this was no ordinary rock, but this was and is a "smitten" Rock. The water was not available until the Rock was smitten (John 7:37-39).

There is another very important truth in this miracle of the river pouring forth from the Rock at Horeb. The Bible says, in I Corinthians 10:4, that the spiritual Rock followed the people in the desert. And the scripture says, *"and that Rock was Christ."* This means that Christ and Him crucified (the smitten Lamb of God) must follow you everywhere, in the wilderness of life, in order for the River, the Holy Spirit, to keep flowing.

We must point out that the Rock (Christ), does not need to be smitten a second time. The work of the Cross has been done once and for all. There will only ever be one Calvary. Jesus Christ is the Source of all life and the Cross is the means by which the life of the Spirit is given.

Moses, from that point on, needed only to speak to the rock and the water would flow (Numbers 20:8). Almost 40 years later, the Israelites would complain again because of the lack of water. This time, however, God told Moses to take the rod, but to only speak to the rock, not to strike it. In anger, because of their constant complaining, Moses lost his temper and struck the rock twice. The Bible says Moses gathered the congregation together before the rock, and he said these words, *"Hear now, ye rebels; must we fetch you water out of this rock?"* (Numbers 20:10). This was a great sin in the eyes of God. He had disobeyed God's directions, taken the situation into his own hands, and it was to cost him dearly. As a typology, it represented Christ being crucified a second time, as if the first time was not sufficient and would have to be repeated.

Most of the modern Church continues to "smite the Rock," committing the same sin as Moses. The work of Calvary has already been done and there is nothing left to be done but to believe. However, whenever a believer in Christ attempts to "do" something to produce their victory, they are, in essence, saying the work of the Cross of Christ was not enough.

Today, we are not to strike the Rock, but we are only to speak to the Rock, and the water, the life giving Spirit, will flow. To "speak" to the Rock is to take the approach that the Cross of Christ is sufficient to meet all my needs. To "strike" the Rock means there needs to be something added to the Cross. In the mind of the believer it should always be the Cross plus nothing. The work on Mount Calvary is a finished work, it needs no improvement (John 19:30).

I would like to make one other observation here. In Exodus 17, immediately after the water started flowing from the Rock, the Bible said, *"then came Amalak, and fought with Israel in Rephidim"* (Exodus 17:8). The evil spirits of darkness always get nervous when the Holy Spirit starts flowing. In fact, there is nothing more threatening to the kingdom of Satan than the power of the Holy Spirit.

A war began between Israel and Amalek. When a person becomes a Christian or is baptized with the Holy Spirit, the believer should understand things may not get easier, as far as the world is concerned. Satan does not like to lose ground and he and his demons may try a counter attack or distraction. Thus the precious time of growing in the Lord may be compromised.

Working in youth ministry for over 20 years, I have seen time after time that as soon as a young person comes to Christ, someone of the opposite sex is likely to come on the scene and begin to take an interest in him or her. An "Amalek" war begins between the flesh and the Spirit, as the tempter tries to steal what God has just done. In fact, the Bible tells us that when the Word is sown in the heart of a person, Satan comes immediately to steal the Word (Mark 4:15). God is a jealous God and He wants to be first in our lives. He wants us to love Him with all of our heart, soul, mind and strength (Deut. 6:5).

Niagara 2001: The River of God

In 2001, we were planning a Niagara Youth Conference in the City of Niagara Falls, NY and over 5,000 young people had registered to attend over their Christmas break. The Conference was themed "River of God." It started to snow on Christmas Eve and continued to snow until the day of the Conference, December 27th. Over 80 inches of snow had fallen and all the roads were closed in and around Niagara Falls, except for one. In many places around Western New York, a state of emergency was declared.

Our ministry staff and board of directors didn't know what to do, as groups were calling our office to ask if the Conference was on or off. I remember going on my knees, with a few of my staff members, to ask the Lord what we should do. As I was praying, it came to my mind what my old Pastor, who God used to lead me to Christ, used to say, "Don't ever cancel what God has ordained." Those words were all I needed and when we finished praying, the others who had gathered with me, had heard the same: not to cancel the Conference! Not knowing how many would even be able to make it, and knowing that some could face dangerous conditions if they decided to come, by faith we said, "It's on."

Our staff and board of directors spent the rest of the day on the phones, directing over 275 churches to find alternate routes to Niagara Falls. It was a great challenge, to say the least, as the snow continued to fall. Miraculously, over 4000 arrived safely for the first night and by the second day, over 5,000 were in attendance. In fact, only 25 groups out of 275 didn't make it and 20 of those were from Buffalo, NY - the closest city to Niagara Falls. The authorities had closed the roads in Buffalo and made it impossible to travel.

As the Conference began, one could only imagine what God was going to do, as the enemy was trying so hard to keep the people away. The war was on, as they say, and what would happen the following three days, at Niagara 2001, would change my life forever. Each day of the Conference was powerful, but on the third day (December 29th), God moved in a way that would change the direction of our ministry forever.

On the morning of December 29, 2001, the Spirit of God brought conviction in the service, as the session theme was "Repentance." Many young people repented of their sins and we could tell God was moving in our midst. As one preacher said, "Repentance always precedes a move of God."

That afternoon, over 5,000 people walked in 84 inches of snow down to Niagara Falls to pray for revival to come to the nations of the world. It was quite a sight, as we used the sound of air horns as a signal for the students to move from one prayer focus to the next. There were so many people that we had to pray in several different groups, as they continued to flow from the Convention Center to the Falls. It was an awesome display and, right in the middle of our prayer time, the sun peeked through the heavy clouds over Niagara Falls, for the first time in several days. We knew God was pleased by the display of faith and endurance through the elements.

That night, we returned to the Convention Center for the evening power session, which turned out to be the night that changed everything. The Spirit of God began to move powerfully through the worship after the message and, as we attempted to close the meeting, God had other plans.

I heard the Lord say to me to call for "Selah," a time of quietness and pause from all activity, and to wait upon God. What I thought would be a minute or two turned into 15 minutes of complete silence, as the leaders of the Conference went prostrate before the Lord. The silence was deafening, as over 5,000 students and leaders waited on the Lord.

The Bible says, *"But they who wait upon the LORD shall renew their strength; they shall mount up with wings as eagles; they shall run, and not be weary, and they shall walk, and not faint"* (Isaiah 40:31).

All of a sudden, in the midst of this delayed time of silence, one student cried out and his voice echoed throughout the Arena. I remember thinking to myself as I prayed, "Don't do that, we are waiting on God to move." However, I quickly discerned that this was the Lord moving through his children. One after the other cried out for God to use them to reach their generation.

Only God knows all that He did in each student that night, but we learned later the importance of that moment for the first student who cried out. A year earlier, at Niagara 2000, Reggie Dabbs (one of the main speakers) had challenged the students to surrender everything and ask God to send them to their schools to reach their lost friends with the Gospel. Students who were willing to accept the challenge were asked to respond with the words, "Lord here am I, send me!" They were invited to come to the altar and give their whole lives to Christ for this purpose. This particular student fought that decision. He knew God was calling him, but he didn't go forward. He missed that moment and had been convicted and troubled by it for the entire year. He knew he had missed God's call.

One year later, however, in the midst of the silence, God spoke to this same young man, "I am giving you a second chance." This time, the young man was not going to miss it.

He cried out in a loud voice, "Lord, here am I, send me!" Wow, what a wonderful God we serve!

The River of God was flowing in the Arena that night and many were experiencing it. One young girl said the presence of God was so strong upon her that she couldn't take it anymore. She got up and began to speak with other tongues. At that point, our worship leader went to the piano and began to play. I learned later that some were offended by the outburst in tongues, and they were actually unnerved by the silence as well. (Remember the words of the scripture, *"Then came Amalek."*)

When God begins to move, the enemy will try to divide. We must be careful to follow the leading of the Spirit, so that everything is done Biblically and in order. We also must not quench nor grieve the Spirit because of fear of what man might think.

As the worship leader led the students in song, the Lord spoke to my heart and He said, "I want you to take Matthew to the cross." My son Matthew (who was five years old at the time), is in a wheel chair, as I mentioned, unable to hold his head up, walk or talk due to the genetic disorder he suffers from.

When Matthew was diagnosed at nine months, my wife and I took on the mindset that we knew God would heal Matthew in heaven one day, so what was 60 years or so, in the light of eternity, to take care of his every need? But in the midst of holding the "Miles Ahead Crusade" in Buffalo in 1999, God spoke to my heart and said these words, "You are not believing right, you believe I can heal Matthew in heaven, but you don't believe I can heal him on earth." He then took me to Mark 9, where a father brings his son to Jesus. The father lacks faith to believe Jesus can heal the boy and Jesus says to the Father, *"all things are possible to him who believeth"* (Mark 9:23). To which the father cried out and said with tears, *"Lord, I believe; help thou mine unbelief"* (Mark 9:24).

I was just like the father in Mark 9 and the Lord wanted me to repent of my unbelief. From that moment, in October of 1999, I knew my wife and I were to believe for Matthew's miracle, even if we had never seen a little boy get out of a wheelchair before. Remember the words that Jesus said to Thomas, who had to see the scars in His hands and side before he would believe, *"Thomas, because thou hast seen me, thou hast believed: blessed are they who have not seen, and yet have believed"* (John 20:29).

At the Conference in 2001, we had a huge wooden cross on the stage and when the Lord said He wanted me to take Matthew to the cross, I knew what He was asking me to do. I instantly responded back to the Lord, "Lord, I don't want to be the center of attention." I sensed God say to me, "Are you more concerned with what the people will think or obeying what I am telling you to do?"

As I was struggling to be obedient to the Lord, I made one last ditch effort to get out of doing what God said to do. As I looked at the altar around the stage, I saw that the students, by the hundreds, had filled the altar and there was no place to get through to the stage. So, I said to the Lord, "I won't even be able to get Matthew through the crowd to the stage." But instantly I was reminded of the woman with the issue of blood, who had to press through the crowds to get to Jesus so she could touch the hem of His garment (Matt. 9:18-22). When that thought came into my mind I knew it was the Lord speaking to me and I immediately went over to my wife, who was sitting with Matthew, and I began to unstrap his legs from the wheelchair. My wife looked at me and said, "What are you doing?" I answered her and said, "I am taking Matthew to the cross."

As I carried little Matty through the crowd, the people saw me coming and they parted like the Red Sea - I had no problem getting him to the stage. I walked up the stairs to the cross, which sat on top of what looked like a mountain (typifying Mount Calvary). I felt like Abraham taking his son, Isaac, up on top of Mount Moriah to sacrifice him. It was a very bizarre feeling, to say the least, but I was a desperate father who would do anything to see my son healed.

I laid Matthew down at the base of the cross, and I began to intercede for his divine healing. Of the 5,000 people in the arena, many began to intercede as well, as they sang a simple chorus over and over again:

"Lord, You are Great, You do miracles so great.
There is no one else like You,
No one else like You,
For You are Great, You do miracles so great."

They sang that song for over 20 minutes. Their faith would not be stopped. What an exhibition it was of a generation crying out for a move of God. Even though Matthew was not healed that night, I knew we had broken through and God was pleased by the faith of so many. We would later receive testimonies, weeks after the Conference, of people who were healed in that service as they interceded for Matthew's healing. Isn't God amazing!

The River was flowing and God was moving. Ezekiel 47:9 says: *every thing shall live, whither the river cometh.* What a mighty God we serve. His Holy Spirit is real and He will ask you to become radical in your faith to see the Mighty River flow in your life as well. God is always moved when His people believe!

That night, December 29, 2001, changed my life forever. It was the night our ministry "crossed the Jordan River," so to speak. There will come a moment, in every Christian's life, where God will ask you to get out of the boat and believe in His miraculous power. Unfortunately, I am afraid most choose to stay in the boat.

The Dead Sea

Every time I travel to Israel, I have life-changing experiences, but something happened on my third trip to the Holy Land that sticks out in my mind - I had an encounter with God at the Dead Sea. Over 40% of this body of water is actually salt and, as a result, there is not one living thing in it, hence the name "Dead Sea."

Also, it is the lowest point on the face of the earth. It is believed to be in the vicinity of where the cities of Sodom and Gomorrah once stood. These cities were destroyed when God rained down fire and brimstone, because of their gross immorality and sexual sin. Everything was destroyed and thousands of lives were judged. This fact may also give you a little more insight into why this Sea is called the Dead Sea.

However, God has a bright future for the Dead Sea. In Ezekiel 47 we are told that the River of God (a type of the Holy Spirit) will begin at the altar of the Temple in Jerusalem, during the time when Christ returns to earth to rule and reign for one thousand years, and flow under the threshold of the house, eastward toward the Dead Sea. At some point this mighty River of God will split with one side going to the Mediterranean (Zech. 14:8) and the other side continuing until it reaches the Dead Sea.

When the River of God reaches the Dead Sea, a transformation is going to happen. The Dead Sea is going to become an "Alive Sea". There will be many fish of all kinds that will live in the Sea that could not survive in the salty waters before. This all signifies the abundance of life that is produced by the

Holy Spirit when a sinner comes to the Cross, repents of his sin and experiences the flow of the "River of God."

In the Millennial Reign of Christ, the Dead Sea will become one of the most sought after fishing resorts in the world. It will continuously remind us all of the power of the Holy Spirit to bring to life that which was dead for so many thousands of years.

You and I need the River of God; the modern Church needs the River of God. Without the River, our services, our programs and our individual lives are lifeless and dead. However, when we believe on the Lord and all that He did on the Cross, and we do not limit the power of the Holy Spirit, we will see life in our churches as well as in our own lives.

The Bible says, in Psalm 46:4, *"There is a river, the streams whereof shall make glad the city of God."* This, again, is speaking of the River we see in Ezekiel 47. Notice what the River does - its streams *"make glad the city of God."* Why?

In Ezekiel 47, we see something very special about this River that will flow in the city of the New Jerusalem. It will be deep enough to swim in and the waters are crystal clear (Ezekiel 47:5). It will have many miracle trees growing along the banks on both sides of the River (Ezekiel 47:7). The trees will perpetually bring forth new fruit because the waters, which come from the Sanctuary of the Temple, nourish them. The Bible says the River begins at the altar. The altar is a type of the Cross, the place of sacrifice. This is a type for us all to see. The fruit on these trees will, no doubt, be luscious fruit growing 12 months of the year and, when the people eat the fruit, it will provide for them, not only food, but also perpetual healing (Ezekiel 47:12).

Remember, in the Bible it was Adam and Eve, in the Garden, who ate from the wrong tree. All of humanity fell at that moment. Some 4,000 years later, God's only Son died on a tree and now, in Ezekiel 47, we see all the glorified saints of God, who have put their faith in Jesus Christ, are, once again, eating from a tree. This time, however, it is not forbidden, bringing death and separation from God, but it is giving them life. It's all about the tree, which represents the Cross. What an amazing God we serve!

Most of the Church today, has ignored the River of God. However, it is this River of the Spirit that brings the power of God to us, as we live our Christian lives. As we have seen in the scriptures we have looked at, you cannot separate the moving of the Holy Spirit from the finished work of Christ on the Cross. The Holy Spirit can only flow in our lives based on our faith being in Christ and Him crucified.

We must forever be about the Cross of Christ and about the Mighty River of God, His Holy Spirit. To neglect the Cross means spiritual death and to neglect the Holy Spirit means spiritual weakness. We must have both all the time - this was and is the plan of God.

Praise the Lord, the Holy Spirit is real! He is still doing what He did in the Book of Acts and He wants to do it for you and for all who will believe His Words.

"And suddenly there came a sound from heaven as of a rushing mighty wind, and it filled all the house where they were sitting. And there appeared unto them cloven tongues, as of fire, and it sat upon each of them. And they were all filled with the Holy Ghost, and began to speak in other tongues as the Spirit gave them utterance." (Acts 2:2-4)

This Mighty River of the Holy Spirit, the Baptism of the Holy Spirit with the evidence of speaking with other tongues, is for all who will believe. It is for you, believer! So, don't delay another moment, jump into the River and experience His Power to live a life centered on the Cross, with Jesus Christ, your Savior. Remember, even 2,000 years later, He is still the same. Hebrews 13:8 says it, *"Jesus Christ is the same yesterday and to day and for ever."*

Endnotes

Chapter 4 – The Fruit Of The Holy Spirit

1. *Hebrew-Greek Key Word Study Bible*. Lexical Aid to the New Testament. Chattanooga, TN: AMG International, Inc. pg 1680.
2. Ibid., pg 1680.
3. Ibid., pg 1768.
4. Ibid., pg 1711.
5. Ibid., pg 1769
6. Assemblies of God: Gifts of the Holy Spirit, The Fruit of the Holy Spirit. [ag.org]
7. *Hebrew-Greek Key Word Study Bible*. Lexical Aid to the New Testament. Chattanooga, TN: AMG International, Inc. pg 1680.

Chapter 5 – The Holy Spirit In The Book Of Acts

Swaggart, Jimmy. *The Cross of Christ Series: The Holy Spirit From Genesis To Revelation*. Baton Rouge, LA: World Evangelism Press, 2006.

Chapter 6 – The Baptism With The Holy Spirit

Swaggart, Jimmy. *The Expositor's Study Bible*. Baton Rouge, LA: Jimmy Swaggart Ministries, 2005. pg 1144.
2. Ibid., pg 20.
3. Ibid., pg 21.

Chapter 7 – The Gifts Of The Holy Spirit

1. Swaggart, Jimmy. *The Cross of Christ Series: The Holy Spirit From Genesis To Revelation*. Baton Rouge, LA: World Evangelism Press, 2006. pg 124.

Chapter 8 – The Revelation Gifts

1. Swaggart, Jimmy. *The Cross of Christ Series: The Holy Spirit From Genesis To Revelation*. Baton Rouge, LA: World Evangelism Press, 2006. pg 132.
2. Vine, W.E. *Vine's Expository Dictionary of New Testament Words*. pg 314.
3. Swaggart, Jimmy. *The Cross of Christ Series: The Holy Spirit From Genesis To Revelation*. Baton Rouge, LA: World Evangelism Press, 2006. pg 137.
4. Ibid., pg 137.

Chapter 9 – The Power Gifts

1. Vine, W.E. *Vine's Expository Dictionary of New Testament Words*. pg 75.

Chapter 10 – The Vocal Gifts

1. Swaggart, Jimmy. *Jimmy Swaggart Bible Commentary: I Corinthians*. Baton Rouge, LA: World Evangelism Press, 1998. pg 419.

Chapter 11 – The "Controversy"

1. *Hebrew-Greek Key Word Study Bible*. Chattanooga, TN: AMG International, Inc.
2. Swaggart, Jimmy. *The Expositor's Study Bible*. Baton Rouge, LA: Jimmy Swaggart Ministries, 2005. pg 2022.

Chapter 13 – The Azusa Street Revival

1. McClung, Grant. Azusa Street & Beyond: 100 Years of Commentary on the Global Pentecostal/Charismatic Movement. Gainesville, FL: Bridge-Logos, 2006. pg 338.
2. Bartleman, Frank. *Azusa Street: The Roots of Modern-day Pentecost*. An Eyewitness Account. Alachua, FL: Bridge-Logos, 1980. pg xx.

3. *Hebrew-Greek Key Word Study Bible*. AMG's Annotated Strong's Greek Dictionary. Chattanooga, TN: AMG International, Inc. pg 2133.

4. Bartleman, Frank. *Azusa Street: The Roots of Modern-day Pentecost*. An Eyewitness Account. Alachua, FL: Bridge-Logos, 1980. pg 61.